Tony Romo

FOOTBALL ● SUPERSTARS

Tiki Barber	Joe Montana
Tom Brady	Walter Payton
Reggie Bush	Adrian Peterson
John Elway	Jerry Rice
Brett Favre	Ben Roethlisberger
Eli Manning	Tony Romo
Peyton Manning	Barry Sanders
Dan Marino	LaDainian Tomlinson
Donovan McNabb	Brian Urlacher

FOOTBALL ⬤ SUPERSTARS

Tony Romo

Clifford W. Mills

CHELSEA HOUSE
An Infobase Learning Company

TONY ROMO

Copyright © 2011 by Infobase Learning

Chelsea House
An imprint of Infobase Learning
132 West 31st Street
New York, NY 10001

Library of Congress Cataloging-in-Publication Data
Mills, Cliff, 1947–
  Tony Romo / Clifford W. Mills.
    p. cm. — (Football superstars)
  Includes bibliographical references and index.
  ISBN 978-1-60413-754-5 (hardcover)
  1. Romo, Tony, 1980-—Juvenile literature. 2. Football players—United States—
Biography—Juvenile literature. 3. Quarterbacks (Football—United States—Biography—
Juvenile literature. I. Title. II. Series.

  GV939.R646M45 2010
  796.332092—dc22
  [B]

                                    2010019328

Chelsea House books are available at special discounts when purchased in bulk quantities for businesses, associations, institutions, or sales promotions. Please call our Special Sales Department in New York at (212) 967-8800 or (800) 322-8755.

You can find Chelsea House on the World Wide Web at http://www.infobaselearning.com

Text design by Erik Lindstrom
Cover design by Ben Peterson and Keith Trego
Composition by EJB Publishing Services
Cover printed by Bang Printing, Brainerd, Minn.
Book printed and bound by Bang Printing, Brainerd, Minn.
Date printed: September 2011
Printed in the United States of America

10 9 8 7 6 5 4 3 2 1

This book is printed on acid-free paper.

CONTENTS

Going into the Panther's Den

Six huge bronze panthers guard the three entrances to the Carolina Panthers' football stadium. Each is painted black with fierce green eyes set into a snarling face with enormous bared teeth. The big cats crouch as if ready to pounce, their large claws gripping 10-foot-high (3-meter-high) pedestals. They seem to closely watch the fans and players who enter the park, now named Bank of America Stadium, at the edge of downtown Charlotte, North Carolina. The panthers are meant to intimidate, like the famous stone lions guarding Chinese imperial palaces, and they do.

On the evening of October 29, 2006, the Dallas Cowboys football team entered the stadium. These guardians of the gates were the least of the Cowboys' worries. They had a quarterback who was starting his first regular season game in the National

7

Football League (NFL). His name was Tony Romo. No big-time college football program had wanted him. He had not been drafted by any professional football team and had been sitting on the Cowboys bench for more than three years as a second- and third-string quarterback. The week before, he had thrown three interceptions as a replacement in the second half against the New York Giants.

The team the Cowboys were about to play, the Carolina Panthers, had defensive linemen who struck fear in the hearts and minds of even the most experienced quarterbacks. They were led by defensive end Julius Peppers, a living legend in the NFL. He is six foot seven inches (201 centimeters) and nearly 300 pounds (136 kilograms), quick and athletic enough to have played basketball for the University of North Carolina. Peppers was the highest paid player in the NFL in 2008, and if an NFL coach could clone only one defensive player, he would probably clone Peppers. One defensive tackle was Kris Jenkins, a 350-pound (159-kg) Pro Bowler who had been called the best defensive lineman in the NFL by the Cowboys' coach, Bill Parcells. Jenkins bench-presses more than 500 pounds (227 kg), so throwing 220-pound (100-kg) quarterbacks to the ground is child's play for him.

Even die-hard fans like Rafael Vela, creator of the "Blue and Silver" Web site, thought that the Cowboys would lose this important game against the powerful and well-coached Panthers. Quarterbacks starting their first games in the NFL against top defenses don't usually win.

A FAMILY IN THE SPOTLIGHT

A few days before, on October 25, 2006, Parcells announced that Tony Romo would start as quarterback, replacing Drew Bledsoe. Writer Mac Engel reports in *Tony Romo: America's Next Quarterback* that half the team thought the move was a good idea, and half didn't. Parcells said at a news conference, "I don't expect perfection, but hopefully he'll give us a little something."

Romo's parents, Ramiro and Joan Romo, immediately had their lives invaded by reporters from most major media outlets—television, radio, print, and the Internet. An unknown quarterback starting for the Cowboys was news, and suddenly everyone wanted to know everything about him.

The Romos live in the small town of Burlington, Wisconsin (with a population of roughly 10,000 people), halfway between Milwaukee, Wisconsin, and Chicago, Illinois. The town was already proud of its most famous citizen: The movie theater had a picture of Tony Romo in the lobby, and "Fred's World's Best Burger" had a Tony Romo table with his picture under glass. A few Cowboys fans had been created in the heart of Green Bay Packer territory.

When *Dallas Morning News* reporter Brad Townsend and many others showed up at the Romos' three-bedroom home—the same house Romo grew up in—Joan Romo served them Danish pastry and showed them childhood photos of her son. She joked, "If I'd had him first, I'd have no other children. He wore me out." The family had not been wealthy. Joan told Townsend, "We had all the needs but probably not all the wants."

She told reporters that her son had always been sports-minded: He devoured books on NFL legends, including quarterback John Unitas and coach Vince Lombardi. Joan recalled catching Tony's practice passes with a pillow until Ramiro came home from work. Ramiro still has a crooked pinky from catching them.

Meanwhile, Ramiro also gave interviews. He confessed that he had doubts. He remembered that Tony had lost his first game as a starter in college, at Eastern Illinois University. He said that, at every step of his son's football career, he thought that Tony might have reached the final level. "Every time he's proven me wrong. I'm not going to doubt him anymore."

Their son had accumulated athletic awards over the years, but few of them were on display. Instead, the shelves were filled with family photos. Tony's awards were mostly stored in

When Tony Romo became quarterback for the Dallas Cowboys, he inspired fans in Wisconsin to turn away from the Green Bay Packers and to the Texas team. *Above*, a husband cheers for the Packers while his wife, a Romo fan, boos them in Romo's hometown of Burlington, Wisconsin.

Rubbermaid containers in the basement. Ramiro and Joan had always tried to keep athletics in perspective and treat each of their children equally. Daughters Danielle and Jossalyn were also at the center of their lives. And they hoped that, even if Tony's life was now changed by his becoming the starting quarterback for "America's Team" (as the Cowboys are often called), Tony himself would not change.

In the small East Texas town of Crockett, other members of Romo's family were waiting for Sunday. His grandparents Ramiro Sr. and Felicita Romo were too nervous to be with others on game day. "I thought of how far we've come, not only as a family, but as a people," Ramiro Sr. told *San Antonio Express-News* reporter David Flores in Spanish. "I remembered the hard times in Mexico and how I struggled when I first got here."

Felicita told Flores, "Tony always has been very close to us. He's always been very attentive, loving." She left a message from Scripture on Romo's answering machine just before the game.

TURNING ON THE BRIGHT LIGHTS: NBC SUNDAY NIGHT FOOTBALL

The whole football world would be watching Romo's first start. *Sunday Night Football* had been taken over by the National Broadcasting Company (NBC) a few months before, and ratings were already higher than those for the more famous *ABC Monday Night Football.* More than 17 million viewers would be tuning in.

Broadcasting superstars Al Michaels and John Madden showed a taped interview with Romo before the game. They asked about his recent breakup with a longtime girlfriend, Crystal Kaspar. Their long-distance relationship—she lived in Florida and he in Texas—had not worked out. (In the years to come, the whole world would know much more about his new girlfriends.) He was then asked to do an impersonation of Brett Favre, the Green Bay Packer quarterback that Romo grew up watching. Romo smiled and imitated the throwing motion and facial expressions of one of his heroes, prompting Michaels to say after the taped interview that Romo was a breath of fresh air.

The broadcasters noted that quarterback for the Cowboys was one of the most celebrated and visible positions in sports, along with center fielder for the New York Yankees and center for the Boston Celtics. Only the Yankees were worth more as a brand name than the Cowboys. The pressure on the young quarterback kept increasing.

The singer Pink came on the air just before the kickoff and sang "I've Been Waiting All Day for Sunday Night." Tony Romo had been waiting all his life for this Sunday night. More than 71,000 people rose to their feet, and thousands of flashing cameras lit the kickoff.

LET THE GAME BEGIN

The first quarter was a disaster for the Cowboys. Romo completed two short passes, but then was violently sacked by the overpowering Kris Jenkins. Panther running back DeShaun Foster scored a touchdown on a one-yard run after a long drive. Then one of Romo's passes was intercepted by cornerback Chris Gamble on a play in which no receiver was open. The smart play would have been to throw the ball out of bounds. Journalist Mark Maske in *War Without Death* writes that, when Romo reached the sideline, Parcells barked, "You're not going to last long doing that!" Tight end Jason Witten tried to reassure Romo, who replied, "Everything's under control." Witten would later say that Romo never loses his cool. But Romo had now thrown four interceptions in less than three quarters. It was a shaky start in a job that demanded instant results.

The Panthers' Steve Smith scored a touchdown on the next play after the interception. For only the second time in his long coaching career, a Parcells team was behind 14-0 in the first quarter.

Parcells often compared football to boxing. He knew that some teams and quarterbacks would, like some boxers, collapse after being hit early and hard. Winners were people who fought back after taking a hard punch, people who didn't let their mistakes keep them down. The coach knew he would find out a great deal about his young quarterback in the next few minutes.

Romo fought back. He responded by driving his team 47 yards in nine plays, throwing a perfect touchdown pass to Witten. His receiver was covered well by a defender, but Romo threw the pass to Witten's left shoulder, where only the tall tight end could catch it. Soon after his defense got the ball back to him, Romo directed a six-minute drive that covered 14 plays and 68 yards, resulting in a field goal. The score was 14-10 at halftime—the Cowboys had climbed back into the fight.

A SECOND HALF TO REMEMBER

Late in the third quarter, Dallas was pinned deep in its own territory. The Cowboys had 18 yards to go for a first down. Romo rifled a pass to receiver Terry Glenn, who had found a seam (an area where pass coverage is weaker) on the left side. The 22-yard pass was complete for a first down, and the Cowboys were out of trouble. Later in the drive, on a third down with 12 yards to go for a first down, Romo sidestepped a vicious pass rush from Peppers and Jenkins to complete a 16-yard pass to Witten in the middle of the field. A Dallas field goal made it 14-13.

Romo was showing that he had four key qualities that define successful NFL quarterbacks: vision of the entire field, a quick release of the pass, accurate throws, and mobility. He was finding the right receiver after looking at several alternatives in a matter of split seconds. He was throwing quick and accurate passes. And he was moving just enough behind his offensive line that he avoided being tackled by the onrushing defensive linemen and linebackers. His mobility was so good that he actually ran for two first downs in the game. He was like a boxer slipping punches, making his opponent miss. How much these qualities are taught and how much they are natural is a matter of debate. The important new fact was that Romo had all four in game conditions. He was not a "practice wonder," someone who does well in practice but freezes in a game.

As often happens in football, the offense inspired the defense and special teams. The Panthers quarterback, Jake Delhomme, was an experienced and proven team leader. It was he, however, and not Romo who began to make key mistakes. Fumbles and interceptions led to three Cowboy touchdowns by running backs Julius Jones and Marion Barber. The Cowboys scored 25 points in the fourth quarter, and won the game 35-14. By the end, many Panther fans had left, and virtually all of the Cowboy fans were on their feet cheering wildly. Romo had completed 24 of 36 passes for 270 yards, a performance that earned him the "Rock Star of the Game" award from Madden and Michaels. A star was indeed born that night.

MORE BRIGHT LIGHTS

Romo came to the postgame news conference wearing a faded and sleeveless T-shirt with the name "Burlington" on it. He has said that he will wear that shirt under his silver-and-blue No. 9 Cowboy uniform until it falls apart.

One of the first things Romo did was thank the man he replaced, Drew Bledsoe: "Drew actually came up to me before

HOW HARD IS IT TO BE AN NFL QUARTERBACK?

Writer George Plimpton once wrote in his book *Paper Lion* that pro quarterbacks are braver and smarter than most people realize. Plimpton should know. He was a good but not exceptional athlete who talked the NFL's Detroit Lions into letting him play quarterback in a practice game. He trained and prepared with the team for weeks. Finally, the day to play came. On his first play, he moved too slowly and his own teammate knocked him down. He lost his balance on the second play because the action was happening so quickly. On the third play, he finally threw a pass, well over the head of the receiver. Fans thought a professional clown had been brought in to amuse them. Plimpton was trying his hardest. He was humiliated.

Quarterbacks multitask with a vengeance. They turn ideas into actions. A quarterback receives a play in the form of a word-and-number code from his coaches through his helmet headset and then gives the play to the team in a huddle. He then chooses the snap count—the word that triggers the offense to go into action.

the game [and] said he was rooting for me. . . . I wouldn't be here if it weren't for Drew." He went on, "I can't put into words the feeling of getting it [the win] done. . . . I was anxious just like Bill [Parcells] to see what we were going to do out there tonight."

He knew that he was part of a team. In a sport like baseball, a player doesn't need his teammates as much as in football, where no one succeeds without key plays from fellow team members. Players go through so much physical, mental, and emotional effort during a game that they bond, much as

When he leads the team to the line of scrimmage (the line on the field where the play begins), he starts to "read" or interpret the defense: How many defenders are "in the box"? These are usually defensive linemen and linebackers, often three or four of each, nearest to him across the line. He also needs to see whether other defensive players, the cornerbacks and safeties, are lining up near his receivers or farther away. He will assess whether the called play puts his team at an advantage or a disadvantage. Are five defensive backs waiting to cover four receivers? That disadvantage is crucial, and the play may need to be changed at the line—an "audible."

Once the ball is snapped, everything becomes a blur. No one player can keep track of all that is happening. Confusion spreads. But one person has to know more than the others—the quarterback. He has to keep reading the defense until the ball leaves his hand as a pass or a handoff to a runner. And then the process starts all over again, as many as 60 times a game. Only a person with extraordinary gifts and training survives.

Tony Romo's first game as quarterback for the Dallas Cowboys started off as a disaster as the Carolina Panthers managed to intercept one of his passes. Romo, however, remained calm and staged a comeback in the second half, leading his team to a 35-14 victory.

soldiers or firefighters or police officers do. They know they win or lose because of each other.

Football is often a series of one-on-one contests and wrestling matches that get little attention. That night, offensive lineman Marc Colombo fought Julius Peppers to a draw, and Peppers had not sacked Romo. Witten, Romo's best friend and roommate when the team traveled, had made difficult catches in the middle of the field while being hounded by a defender ready to flatten him. Terrell Owens, a very controversial and outspoken receiver, had caught nine passes and made tacklers miss after several catches.

Coach Parcells knew he had seen something special. He said, "We haven't been having a lot of fun around here. They're having fun right now. That's the thing I enjoy the most. When I see the faces of the players." No one was having more fun than Romo.

Cowboys' owner Jerry Jones was impressed. "We expected—I expected—to pay some price for that being his first start. He just played beyond my expectations throughout the game." Mark Maske wrote in *War Without Death* that "the Cowboys, for the first time in years, just might have found a quarterback capable of being The Guy for them for a long, long time."

FEELING IT THE DAY AFTER

Bryan Nielsen was the sports editor for the paper in Charleston, Illinois, the home of Romo's college, Eastern Illinois University. He called Romo the next day but had no expectations that the quarterback could make time for a small newspaper now that he was the talk of the football world. He need not have worried. Romo returned his call, saying, "I have a special place in my heart for Charleston, and that's never going to change."

Romo described his sudden fame to Nielsen. "You don't realize sometimes how easy it is to go to the mall without people knowing who you are. It goes with the territory, but I'm more of a small-town guy." He went on to say that he had received many calls and text messages as a result of being on national television. He knew, however, that instant fame meant instant criticism. "You know as well as I do that you can go from the penthouse to the outhouse in a hurry." Over the next few years, Romo would know both places. But his nature and upbringing had prepared him for the storm-tossed hero's journey he had now begun.

A Big Athlete
in a Small Town

Tony Romo is proud of his Hispanic heritage. Romo's grandfather, Ramiro Sr., was born in 1933 in the mining town of Múzquiz in the State of Coahuila. The town is in northeastern Mexico and is surrounded by spectacular mountain views. When he was 11 years old, his family traveled the short distance to San Antonio, Texas, to begin life in America. When his mother died several years later, Ramiro Sr. was devastated. His brother persuaded him to move north to help get away from the pain of that loss. He arrived in Racine, Wisconsin, in November 1951.

Racine is a port city on the western shore of Lake Michigan, south of Milwaukee and north of Chicago. It is an industrial center with many kinds of jobs, and Ramiro Sr. began to look for work in factories and gas stations. He found the northern winters a shock—the icy wind off the lake made him think about returning to the sun of Texas or Mexico.

But he soon met an attractive young woman named Felicita Rios and decided to stay in Wisconsin. Her parents were from Mexico but had emigrated to Robstown, Texas. She was born there in 1934, and her family had moved to Racine when she was 12. Ramiro and Felicita fell in love and married in 1955. Ramiro Jr., Tony's father, was born soon after, and another son, Mustafa John, was adopted. The family made do with what they had and adapted to a place with only a small Hispanic community.

THE ROMOS MOVE TO BURLINGTON

Ramiro Jr. grew up a gifted athlete. He played the two sports that he loved, basketball and soccer, at St. Bonaventure High School in Racine. He became a strong young man in every sense of the word. When he was in his teens, he met and fell in love with a lively and outgoing young woman named Joan Jakubowski; they married when he was 18 and she was 19. Joan's parents had German and Polish ancestors, so the Romos' children would have many cultures to draw on as part of their family's story.

Joan and Ramiro soon had two daughters—Danielle and Jossalyn. Then, while Ramiro was serving a five-year term in the United States Navy and based in San Diego, California, they had a son. He was born on April 21, 1980, at a naval base and was named Antonio Ramiro Romo. He was soon called "Tony."

When Ramiro was discharged from the navy, he and Joan decided to move the family back to Wisconsin. In July 1982, when Danielle was six, Jossayln was four, and Tony was two, the family settled in a small town west of Racine, named Burlington. Homesick settlers from New England had named the town after Burlington, Vermont. It was now known as "Chocolate City U.S.A" after a large Nestlé factory was built there in 1966.

Ramiro Jr. had always been good with his hands, and he became a carpenter. He built an 1,100-square-foot house on a small lot near the Burlington Cemetery—a quiet spot. The family still lives there today.

GETTING INTO EVERYTHING

The Romos were strict but loving parents and tried to eat together every night and go to church every Sunday. Young Tony often was a shepherd in the Christmas nativity play. Video games were discouraged. If any of the kids wanted to play, they had to go to a friend's house.

Since Joan and Ramiro's only son was also the baby of the family, he was given a little more leeway than his older sisters. Like many last-born sons with older sisters, he was more rebellious than his siblings. In one family story, he managed to get his oldest sister, Danielle, to sign his mother's name to a school absence slip. Also like many brothers with older sisters, he was social, outgoing, and competitive.

He was competitive about everything. He loved contests and stories about them. He also liked to watch his father play basketball at the city gym. Ramiro added a basketball hoop to the driveway when Tony was five or six, but he didn't want to lower the 10-foot regulation height to make shooting baskets easier for his son. Writer Mac Engel in *Tony Romo* reports that Ramiro said, "The little guy would be out there for two hours and make two baskets."

When Joan took a job in the clubhouse at the local golf course, Tony found another interest. When he was eight, his parents bought him a small set of golf clubs for Christmas. He went outside that cold December morning and teed up a golf ball on an empty lot. Joan told Ramiro that she was worried her son was going to hit a neighbor's house. Ramiro told her not to worry: "He'll miss it." Instead, Tony hit the ball some 70 yards (64 meters) into a neighbor's living room.

Felicita and Ramiro Romo Sr. (*above*) are dedicated supporters of their grandson. Ramiro Sr., who immigrated to the United States when he was 11 years old, believes that Tony's success is an example of the opportunities available to everyone in America.

Soon he was playing golf before school, arriving in class with clothes wet from the morning dew. He sometimes followed his father onto the golf course and would hit his first shot at the spot where his father's tee shot had landed. Golf was something the whole family could do together.

Baseball was another early interest. When he was nine, Tony joined Little League as a shortstop and pitcher for the Burlington Minis. He even asked for a set of bases for Christmas. His strength as a baseball player soon proved to be as a catcher, however. Like another famous NFL quarterback who played the position, New England Patriot Tom Brady, Romo was deadly accurate with throws while coming up from a crouch to gun down runners. And, like Brady, he found he liked to be at the center of the action—a catcher has to be tough, smart, and a natural team leader.

Although Burlington didn't have a youth football league, Tony organized football games during recess at Waller Elementary School. His teams rarely lost, partly because he made up plays that could fool the other team. He always wanted to figure out a way to win.

Despite his interest in golf and baseball, his middle school years were filled with basketball and soccer, the two games his father played and excelled at. One of his coaches was Scott Hoffman, who told Brad Townsend of the *Dallas Morning News* that Tony "was smart, smarter than most coaches. He would always look for shortcuts, how to finish drills the quickest. Tony always wanted to get to game day."

EARLY TEENAGE ROMO

As a teenager, Tony was as normal off the playing field as he was extraordinary on it. He could be the annoying younger brother: When he found Danielle's diary, Joan told reporters, "that nearly started World War III." And like many teenagers, he had many part-time jobs. He worked in a hospital and a restaurant and also for his father, who had become a construction supervisor. His friend Paul Bender has told reporters that Romo liked to enlist help from his friends, turning tough jobs like moving massive piles of building supplies into a competition.

Like author Mark Twain's character Tom Sawyer, who famously gets people to help him paint a fence white, Romo knew how to motivate people. Tom Sawyer is portrayed as adventurous and playful, with a natural ability to lead. But he has a slightly rebellious streak that made him mostly good and partly bad. He needed to be civilized, and the women in his life would try to get him to settle down. Just as Sawyer liked to escape into the wild for adventures, Romo would escape into the wild of sports.

Romo was not exactly a model student, but he managed a B average, often cramming in study and homework time on the bus to school. His high school wood-shop teacher joked that he would pass Romo only if he would agree never to take another shop class.

GETTING SERIOUS ABOUT SPORTS

In his teen years, Tony was still interested in sports. He studied sports films and books, and watched the VHS videotape of basketball legend "Pistol" Pete Maravich until the copy burned out. He then burned out a second copy, and a third. When he watched sports on television, he became a student of the mechanics of each player he liked.

Psychologist Howard Gardner writes in *Frames of Mind* that young people with "bodily intelligence" can watch others and imitate their actions precisely. Romo seems to have been born such a mimic. Gardner writes that athletes have some qualities that are innate, meaning that they are born with them, and some that they develop through practice. Innate characteristics include hair-trigger coordination and strength. The ones that need to be developed are poise—the ability to move well under pressure—and control. Control and coordination lead to good timing, a rhythm that athletes feel and that is important to their performance.

At some point, writer Engel notes, Romo got a sports version of "the talk" from his father. His father told him he had a natural and innate gift for sports, but to excel he was going to have to practice more and work hard. His parents were never going to force him to do anything, and they were going to love him no matter what happened. Nevertheless, he would have to make a decision about how good he wanted to be.

Romo's parents helped him become an athlete in many ways. One small and simple one was to buy pizza and soda and let their son and his friends watch sports movies in the basement. At some point, the movie *The Natural* became Romo's favorite. It is a famous film about a fictional baseball player, Roy Hobbs, who wore uniform No. 9. Romo would choose that number as a Cowboy.

BECOMING AN ALL-AROUND JOCK IN HIGH SCHOOL

Romo arrived at Burlington High School as a well-known athlete. He immediately tried out and made the school soccer team, but he quit partly because the team had trouble fielding a full roster of players. Also, the sport and its constant running no longer seemed to interest him fully. He talked to his father about trying out for the football team, now two weeks into its training. His father asked, "Which position?" Romo replied, "quarterback." He made the team and soon was the starting quarterback for the freshman "B" team.

One day that spring, golf coach Bill Berkholtz watched in amazement as Tony played a pickup match with the No. 3 varsity tennis player. A ninth grader with little tennis experience should not be able to beat an experienced older player. Tony crushed him. Still, tennis lost out to golf for Tony's attention. He had loved the game since he was very young, and his older sister Jossalyn was on a golf team as well. Berkholtz saw that Romo had plenty of natural talent, and he encouraged Romo to be patient on the golf course. The coach would later say that if Romo had made golf his full-time sport, he could have become a professional.

Basketball was Romo's winter sport in high school, and he was a star point guard by his second season. One night during

Romo's sophomore year, first-year coach Steve Berezowitz waited nervously as the team gathered in a heavy snowstorm to go to a big game against East Troy. Romo hadn't arrived when the bus needed to leave, so it set off without him. Ramiro had been delayed getting home because of the snow, so Tony took off on his bicycle, heading for East Troy—about 15 miles (24 kilometers) away. Luckily, Ramiro saw Tony on his bike and gave him

A SPORTS FANTASY FOR THE AGES: *THE NATURAL*

One of the most famous athletes of all time is fictional: Roy Hobbs. He was created by novelist Bernard Malamud, and the 1984 movie based on his book *The Natural* was directed by Barry Levinson and starred Robert Redford as Hobbs.

Hobbs is a small-town Midwesterner on a quest to be the best baseball player who ever lived. He has all the natural gifts for greatness and is armed with a hero's "sword"—a bat named "Wonderboy"—carved from a tree split by lightning. But, at age 19, he is shot by a deranged woman, barely survives, and disappears. Sixteen years later, he finally makes it to the Major Leagues, with the fictional New York Knights. He single-handedly turns them from losers to winners, hitting legendary home runs at key moments. He can literally knock the cover off the ball, generating fireworks with his accomplishments.

Three forces—success, failure, and fame—fight for his body and soul. They are embodied in three women: His high school girlfriend, Iris Gaines (played by Glenn Close), brings him success; the wife of the Knights' owner, Memo Paris (Kim Basinger), pulls him toward failure; and Harriet Bird's (Barbara Hershey) obsession with famous players almost kills him.

a ride the rest of the way. The coach told writer Mac Engel, "We would have been dead without him. We won in overtime."

A LATE START FINDING GLORY ON THE FOOTBALL FIELD

Romo did not start as quarterback for the Burlington High Demons during the 1995 season, because early on in his

The movie peaks with Hobbs bleeding from the old gunshot wound (he had been shot by a silver bullet that stayed in his body) but hitting the winning home run in the most important game of his life. Iris and Hobbs's son (unknown to him before that game) watch from the stands and cheer. The final scene shows Hobbs, Iris, and their son playing catch in a sunlit field surrounded by high grass. His quest has brought glory, suffering, and, finally, peace.

One of the most famous lines in the movie is spoken by Iris, who says that people have two lives, "the life they learn with and the life they live after that." Many athletes say their lives are about second chances, about the lives they are leading after they have learned. Roy Hobbs is an example of a second chance.

Interestingly, the novel ends with Roy striking out. Many critics dismissed the movie and its "Hollywood ending," but the film has endured as an American classic, especially for sports fans. Several sports critics aware of Romo's fascination with the movie have compared his romantic relationships to those of Roy Hobbs. Romo's supporters hope he will find his Iris and not be trapped by a Memo Paris.

For Burlington High School football coach Steve Gerber (*above*), Romo stood out from other players because he was able to improvise on the field and visualize plays. Romo's natural leadership abilities and athleticism allowed him to shine in several sports, and he competed year round in high school.

sophomore season, a broken finger limited his play. The team had a 9–3 record in its conference, but football coach Steve Gerber remembers one play that Romo made: "There was one time this kid had him [Romo] sacked, and he changed hands … and threw it left-handed 20 yards." Romo was already showing that some of his most dramatic plays were not scripted ones. He could improvise. Gerber had suggested that Romo wear No. 16 as a tribute to one of Romo's heroes, San Francisco 49ers quarterback Joe Montana. Like Montana, he was making the most of his gifts, seeing the whole field and helping his coach by suggesting what was working and not working on the field. Gerber told reporter Brad Townsend that "the normal high school quarterback that I worked with—that kid would see one side of the field. . . . Tony was one of those kids who could go left to right and back to the left."

Romo was still not the starter for the Demons at the beginning of his junior-year season in 1996. At halftime of the team's second game, however, he was put in and the team never looked back. In his senior year, Burlington High (with 1,100 students) was put into a tougher football conference, with much larger schools from Racine and Kenosha. The team struggled in Romo's senior season in 1997, going 3–6. But Romo was a standout: He was named to the Wisconsin Football Coaches All-Star first team.

FINDING THE RIGHT COLLEGE

Unlike many young star athletes, Romo had not attended expensive football camps—his family didn't know much about them. He had not concentrated on one sport—he loved many sports and liked to change them with the seasons. So, no Division I football team had him on its radar.

The NCAA divides colleges and universities that have varsity football programs into Division I, II, and III, depending on enrollments, stadium size, numbers of scholarships given, and other factors. Division I had two parts, I-A (for the biggest universities) and I-AA (for moderately sized universities and colleges), until 2006, when the labels were changed to Football Bowl Subdivision (FBS) for I-A and Football Championship Subdivision (FCS) for I-AA.

The most logical choice for Romo's college seemed to be the University of Wisconsin–Whitewater. It had a small Division

III football program, and Whitewater wasn't far from home. The choice seemed to be a no-brainer.

But Romo's reputation as a good quarterback had spread. A man named Roy Wittke had become the offensive coordinator for the Eastern Illinois University (EIU) football team, a larger I-AA team with a long football history dating back to 1899. Wittke was always looking for football talent, and when his parents in Racine sent him newspaper articles about the senior quarterback, Wittke knew he had to see Romo for himself. Football season was over, however, so instead he went to a Burlington basketball game. He told Townsend, "Every time a play needed to be made, a big basket or a rebound, Tony was in the middle of it. You sensed that he had something special about him." Wittke was impressed.

Eastern Illinois' head football coach Bob Spoo was doubtful. Romo was not especially big or fast nor had he played at a large high school. He told Engel: "I have to admit, I really didn't think he could do anything. Coach Wittke was the guy who had to convince me."

Romo visited the Charleston campus of Eastern Illinois University in January 1998. Wittke told Engel, "What was readily apparent was that Tony was a gym rat. He was a serious competitor. He played several sports. He was an overall athlete—that was what I tried to sell Coach Spoo." Eventually, EIU offered Romo a partial scholarship. Football players are almost always given full scholarships, but it was better than nothing. He would be going to college. He was ready to move away from the security of home and test himself against bigger and faster opponents and the wider world of an out-of-state college.

College Days

Tony Romo arrived at Eastern Illinois University in the fall of 1998. EIU is a medium-sized university of roughly 12,000 students on an attractive 320-acre campus in Charleston, Illinois, in the east-central part of the state. The city and university are surrounded by rich green farms and prairie—millions of bushels of corn and soybeans are grown and harvested each year. It is indeed the land of Abraham Lincoln—the president's father, Tom, once lived in a log cabin only a few miles from where the campus now stands.

EIU has been called the "Cradle of Coaches." Remarkably, three recent NFL coaches are EIU graduates: Mike Shanahan (Redskins and formerly the Broncos), Sean Payton (Saints), and Brad Childress (Vikings). It may be a Division I-AA program, but EIU pursues football excellence.

College and pro football coaches tend to be divided on the importance of strategy versus talent. Some feel that the winning team simply has the most talented players—faster, bigger, stronger, and better at throwing, running, catching, blocking, and tackling. Recruiting and drafting, along with motivating, are then the keys to success. Other coaches believe that strategy is most important—how you use the players, what "schemes" and "systems" a team uses. The most successful coaches at the college and pro levels blend the two approaches. Shanahan, Payton, and Childress have stressed both talent and system.

GETTING REDSHIRTED

EIU football coach Bob Spoo looked at his quarterback talent in the fall of 1998 and must have been pleased. EIU had a proven starting quarterback, Anthony Buich, who would later play pro ball in the Arena Football League. One of Romo's competitors for the role of backup quarterback, Julius Davis, was a gifted all-around athlete perfectly suited for EIU's "run-first" offense (using running plays more than passing plays). So Spoo and Wittke discussed the possibility of switching Romo to tight end, a position where he could block for runners as well as catch.

After watching him play, Spoo "redshirted" Romo. That meant Romo's first year as a full football team member would be delayed a year. Romo looked as if he wasn't ready to make the next step beyond high school. He was no longer clearly the best athlete on the field. The college game moved faster. Some professional football players have said that the transition from high school to college football is even harder than that from college to professional football. Spoo told writer Mac Engel, "He really didn't have the best arm. And, I think more than anything else, he didn't know what it took just yet in terms of the work or dedication."

Joan and Ramiro Romo received many phone calls from their disheartened son, who was now wondering whether he should try to excel in basketball instead of football. But he had found a Methodist church in Charleston that gave him consolation. And he was lucky—he had someone else looking out for him on campus, a guardian angel. Roy Wittke felt responsible for Romo.

One winter night, Romo had reached the finals of a three-on-three basketball tournament on campus and skipped a scheduled study hall. Wittke came down on him hard, making him attend a 6 A.M. disciplinary workout the next day. Romo responded well to the push. He worked harder.

Romo's first year as a full member of the EIU team was in 1999, his second year as a student. He had worked hard enough to become the backup quarterback, beating out Davis, and when Buich was injured, Romo started in the game against Central Florida. The team lost 31-21, and went on to a 2–10 season. Romo played in three games, just enough to give him a taste of what he needed to do to succeed the next year. Wittke told Townsend, "There are a thousand Tony Romos out there, a lot of guys with potential. But he did something about it."

During the summer, Romo drove to Terre Haute, Indiana, to watch the Indianapolis Colts train. He watched quarterback Peyton Manning's every move. Romo put his visual learning skills and bodily intelligence to good use. He also noticed that Manning stayed after practice to correct any mistakes he had made. The best quarterbacks make mistakes, but they try very hard not to make them twice.

AT LAST, STARTING QUARTERBACK

For the 2000 season, Romo was finally the starting quarterback. When he walked into EIU's 10,000-seat O'Brien Stadium wearing No. 17 on his blue-and-gray uniform for the home opener, he took command. He won his first two games, including a 72-0 blowout of Kentucky Wesleyan. The team went on to have a winning record and reach the I-AA play-offs. EIU lost to the No. 1 team, Montana, 45-13, but the Panthers had proved they belonged among the top I-AA teams in the country. Romo threw for more than 2,500 yards and 27 touchdowns, an impressive performance for his first year as a starter. He was named the Ohio Valley Conference (OVC) Player of the Year. He had arrived.

In 2001, Romo did even better. He led the team to a 9–1 record, including being unbeaten in the OVC. One of the season's key games was a thriller over Tennessee State University in late October. With less than three minutes remaining in the game, Romo drove his team the length of the field, making two third-and-long plays that kept the drive alive. Bill Besenhofer's short field goal with no time left won the game. Romo was brilliant, completing passes for 381 yards and three touchdowns.

Romo's statistics in 2001 were not quite as flashy as in 2000—he completed 138 of 207 passes for 2,068 yards, with 21 touchdown passes—but his team was better. It won a share of the OVC championship. EIU lost an offensive battle to Northern Iowa, 49-43, in the play-offs, even though Romo threw five touchdowns and passed for 386 yards. Again, Romo was named the OVC Player of the Year.

In 2002, his senior year, Romo kept improving. Many other players level off in college by their senior year, but not Romo. The EIU Panthers started the season playing two dominant I-A teams, the University of Hawaii and Kansas State University. Romo threw for four touchdowns and 319 yards against Hawaii in the opening game. He completed 23 of 35 passes against Kansas State. Even though the Panthers fell short in both games, Romo proved he could play against powerhouse teams.

In the homecoming game against powerful Eastern Kentucky, Romo made a play that is still talked about at EIU. Losing 24-19 with 43 seconds left, EIU got the ball on its own 25-yard line. Romo had no time-outs. The situation was almost hopeless. He hit two perfect sideline passes to get near midfield. Romo then fired a 45-yard strike to a receiver who

Romo arrived at Eastern Illinois University on a partial football scholarship, but the coaches questioned whether he would be able to make the transition to college-level athletics. With his status on the football team in jeopardy, Romo pushed himself to improve and became the starting quarterback in 2000.

was tackled at the Eastern Kentucky eight-yard line. There was barely time for one more play. Romo was rushed hard as he went back to pass. He dodged one tackler, then another. He began to weave his way up the field as every Eastern Kentucky player converged on him. No one thought he could get through the entire defense and make it to the goal line. But he did—diving into the end zone, just inside the marker. The Panthers won the game, 25-24. It was a Hollywood ending and the start of an EIU legend.

RECEIVING THE WALTER PAYTON AWARD

Romo finished his remarkable senior season with 33 touchdowns, completing 237 of 363 passes for a 65.3 percent completion average and 2,950 yards. His team ended up 8–3 but lost again in the play-offs to Western Illinois, 48-9. Despite the loss, the season was another success, and Romo was voted the OVC Player of the Year for the third straight year, something that had never happened before. For his college career, he had 84 touchdowns, smashing the previous EIU career record of 75 held by Sean Payton.

Because of these extraordinary achievements, Romo was among the final candidates for the prestigious Walter Payton Award, given to the best offensive player at an I-AA university or college. In Chattanooga, Tennessee, with his father and mother in the audience, it was announced that the winner was Tony Romo. Joan's eyes filled with tears. They had attended almost all of his games for the past four years.

Bob Spoo got up and spoke. He congratulated his quarterback:

Walter Payton exemplified what dedication and commitment can accomplish. Tony is a classic example of what can be achieved by following Payton's qualities. Tony earned the respect of his teammates by his work ethic. No matter how much individual success he achieved, he still was one of the hardest working players right up to his final collegiate game. That work ethic and leadership resulted in his teammates expecting to succeed.

The Walter Payton Award is the one trophy that occupies a central place in the Romo household, on top of the entertainment center. It meant so much to the family because Payton meant so much to football.

SEARCHING FOR A CAREER

At some point during his senior year, Romo thought for the first time that he could play in the NFL. His father wasn't so sure. He knew that his son had not attended a Division I-A university and would be overlooked by many NFL teams as they drafted players.

Romo had been a communications major at Eastern Illinois, and sports broadcasting was a career option. Mike Bradd, an EIU communications professor and the football play-by-play announcer, had taught Romo in a television production class. Bradd told reporter Townsend that Romo was a good student and recalled one class: "It was live studio production. For a lot of students, that's difficult. You have to multitask. Tony sits down, puts the headset on, and it was 'OK, you do this, you need to do that.' He's keeping track of eight different people at once."

The communications skills Romo had developed at EIU would prove to be invaluable. He may have reasoned that very few get the chance to play pro football and a broadcasting career could wait. When he was invited to take part in the 2003 National Invitational Camp, better known as "the Combine," he jumped at the chance.

GETTING TESTED: THE NFL COMBINE

Every February, some 300 college players are invited to Indianapolis, Indiana, for the Combine—several days of physical and mental tests and interviews by NFL coaches, scouts, and executives. Each team rates a player according to whether and when he should be drafted.

The Combine has been called a meat market, a livestock judging competition, a job fair, a beauty pageant, a football convention, a sales meeting for sports agents, and many other names. Still, it is important: How players perform at the Combine often affects when they will be drafted, and how high they go in the draft affects their salary and their future.

WALTER PAYTON

The Walter Payton Award is named after an extraordinary man. Coach and television commentator Mike Ditka called Payton the best football player he had ever seen at any position.

Born on July 25, 1954, in Columbia, Mississippi, Walter Payton grew up with many interests, like Tony Romo. Payton loved to play the drums in jazz and rock bands, was an active member at church, and an athlete in several sports. He didn't play football in high school until his older brother Eddie had graduated, so he wouldn't compete for a running back position with him.

The first time Payton touched a football in a high school game, he ran for 65 yards. He broke many regional high school records, but he was not seriously recruited by many of the larger universities in the Southeastern Conference because he was African American at a time before civil rights were fully in place. So, he went to Division I-AA Jackson State University in Jackson, Mississippi. He was nothing short of sensational.

On January 28, 1975, he was drafted by the NFL's Chicago Bears. For the next 13 seasons, he proved to be one of the most

Romo arrived at the RCA Dome in Indianapolis in the last week of February 2003. He was assigned a number, like all the other players, most in dark gray sweatshirts. He was weighed and given a physical, including a drug-screening test. He then had to perform in the 40-yard dash, vertical and broad jumps, a 20-yard shuttle run, a bench press, and throwing drills, among other physical tests. Romo's time in the 40-yard dash was 5.0 seconds, and his vertical leap was 30 inches. Both are unimpressive by NFL standards.

explosive running backs in the sport's history. His strength and toughness were legendary. He didn't run out of bounds to avoid tacklers—he ran at them. When he scored a touchdown, he didn't celebrate. Instead, he handed the ball to one of his offensive linemen. He often said they did all the work.

He missed one game in 13 years, and only then in his rookie season when a coach made him sit out with an ankle injury. When he retired after the 1987 season, he had rushed for 16,726 yards, a record only surpassed by Emmitt Smith in October 2002. When he was inducted into the Pro Football Hall of Fame, he chose his son Jarrett, then 12, to introduce him. Jarrett said, "Not only is my dad an exceptional athlete, he's my biggest role model and best friend."

Payton was diagnosed with liver cancer at the age of 45, and his name was put on a list of organ donor recipients. He refused to move up the list because of his fame. He later refused a liver transplant near the end of his life because to do so would mean costing another person his or her life. He died at age 45.

Romo's outstanding performance as EIU's quarterback earned him the 2002 Walter Payton Award. Named after a football legend, the accolade is given out every year to the best offensive player in Division I-AA college football.

Jim Hess, a scout with the Dallas Cowboys, watched Romo. He noticed that the young quarterback pitched in to help others with their drills, throwing to receivers for hour after hour. Engel writes that Hess approached Romo and said, "Man, your arm is going to fall off." Romo replied, "I'm fine. This isn't going to bother me."

All players are given the Wonderlic Personnel Test, a 50-question intelligence test with a 12-minute time limit. The Wonderlic scores are like SATs—players get labeled by them. Romo's score was reported as a 37, placing him among the top 5 percent of quarterbacks in the period from 1996 to 2006. His mental skills were testing higher than his physical ones.

One of football's great talent evaluators is a man named Gil Brandt. He wrote a card on Romo that read, "Looks good moving around and throwing the ball. Great job with the media." It was praise, but faint praise. The Cowboys' draft card said that Romo was competitive, smart, and had heart. But when draft day came a few weeks later, no team selected Romo. Carson Palmer, Byron Leftwich, Kyle Boller, and Rex Grossman were drafted in the first round. Some other quarterbacks chosen were Dave Ragone, Brian St. Pierre, Seneca Wallace, Kliff Kingsbury, and Gibran Hamdan. Only Palmer and Leftwich have achieved starting quarterback success over a period of years. Many are no longer playing professional football. Clearly, teams had a long way to go in evaluating quarterbacks.

GETTING SIGNED BY THE COWBOYS

Two men had strongly considered drafting Romo: Mike Shanahan and Sean Payton. Both had been quarterbacks at Eastern Illinois and knew the competition in the Ohio Valley Conference was better than many people thought. Shanahan had played at EIU in the 1970s and almost died after injuring a kidney because of a vicious hit on the practice field. He was head coach of the Denver Broncos. Payton had just become an offensive coordinator and assistant coach for the Cowboys under Bill Parcells.

Coach Shanahan tried hard to sign Romo as an undrafted free agent, but Cowboys' owner Jerry Jones and coaches Parcells and Payton all made recruiting calls to Romo after draft weekend. It was no contest: Romo felt Parcells was a proven winner, and he knew he would learn a great deal from him and from Payton. His beloved grandparents now lived in Texas, and he had even jokingly told his grandmother that he would play for the Cowboys someday. He couldn't disappoint her.

On May 1, 2003, Romo signed a contract for roughly $12,000, which would also cover his room and board expenses at training camp. Of the thousands of young men who play college football each year, he was now among the few hundred who got a chance to play in the NFL. His quest to see how good he could be had landed him in the great state of Texas.

Becoming a
Pro Quarterback

A week after signing his contract, Tony Romo reported to the rookie minicamp in San Antonio, Texas. The minicamp had training sessions for first-year players. Every rookie would be under a microscope, analyzed by the head coach and offensive and defensive coordinators. Coach Bill Parcells was clearly in charge: He liked to show the rookies who was boss. The team's highest draft pick, Terence Newman, had to get Parcells water during breaks. Rookies were not allowed to wear helmets with the famous Dallas Cowboys star. They would have to earn that right.

The coach firmly believed that most players did only what he made them do and did not go beyond that. Michael Lewis writes in *The Blind Side* that Parcells thought some players seemed to want to win more than they actually tried to win:

"What they wanted, deep down, was to keep their jobs, make their money, and go home." He didn't want those kinds of players on his team.

Parcells liked the way Romo had handled the deep disappointment of not being drafted. Parcells told *New York Times* reporter Karen Crouse, "He was clear thinking. . . . I could tell under the gun he's going to be analytical. And that's a good sign, particularly when you have a coach who has a tendency to be emotional under the gun."

Parcells and Romo had something in common: They grew up in a world of sports. In Michael MacCambridge's *America's Game*, Parcells says, "I grew up in an environment where every day you went to the school yard or the playground, and every day you're playing from morning till night to find out who was the best."

THE NEAR-FATAL FLAW

Quarterbacks coach David Lee and offensive coordinator Sean Payton liked what they saw in Romo at minicamp. He released the ball quickly and threw accurately and hard. He had what football experts call "pocket presence," an ability to stay calm in the pocket and move around to buy a little more time before throwing the ball.

On the last day of minicamp, Lee approached Parcells to praise Romo. Parcells, however, told him he didn't like what he saw with the rookie quarterback. He saw a thrower, not a passer. In *Tony Romo*, Mac Engel writes that Parcells said to Lee, "The way he's throwing now, he'll get six balls batted down every ten throws."

The problem was that Romo threw the football only three-quarters of the way to straight overhand. The ball is then released lower than it would be if thrown fully overhand. So, big NFL defensive players would be able to knock down or tip many passes. Professional linemen and linebackers are trained to jump at just the right moment and keep their arms up to distract the quarterback. And a six-foot-five-inch (196-cm) quarterback wouldn't be as affected as one at six-foot-two (188 cm), which is Romo's height. For Parcells, it was a near-fatal flaw.

As they were leaving the field, Romo asked Lee what he needed to do to improve. Lee at first only praised him, but Romo pressed him about what Parcells thought. Finally, Lee told him what Parcells had said. Romo wasn't defensive or devastated: He took the criticism and persuaded Lee to work with him to change his throwing motion. Lee told Engel, "You're talking about changing the way a guy has thrown for however long. That's muscle memory. You can't change that. It takes about 10,000 throws. Maybe a year to do it."

Lee took Romo on as a project. The rookie had a way of making people want to help him. He knew what he didn't know. Some days, they worked together just after dawn, and some days they worked into the night. The goal was to get Romo to throw the ball with a more straight-over-the-top motion, at least 12 inches (30 cm) above where he had been throwing it all his life. Romo threw so many passes that Lee's hands had broken blood vessels, just as Ramiro Romo's hands had years before.

TRAINING CAMP 2003

Several weeks later, the 2003 training camp for the Cowboys began in San Antonio. Lee and Romo had not had enough time to completely change Romo's throwing angle so that it was natural. Lee told Engel, "I was holding my breath for him. . . . Everything he threw was high." Fixing one problem had caused another. Many of Romo's passes were now sailing high over their targets. A quarterback is usually trained to try to hit a receiver "between the numbers" when possible or even at the corner of one of the numbers—in other words, a specific place chest- or shoulder-high.

Romo had a great deal to learn. A quarterback has to be a master of physics, even if he doesn't know it. Author Timothy

Upon entering Cowboys training camp, Romo (*left*) knew when he did not perform at the high standard head coach Bill Parcells (*right*) demanded of his players. Whenever Parcells yelled at him over a botched play, Romo went back onto the field to work on getting it right.

Gay, in *The Physics of Football,* notes that to complete a pass a quarterback has to throw at the right speed, in the right direction, at the right time. He has little room for mistakes: The pass often must be within a half mile per hour of the right speed and .20 seconds of the right time to be completed. The launch angle, the direction the football travels as it leaves the quarterback's hand, must be precise as well.

All quarterbacks must figure out on each play the right speed to throw the ball. The three basic options are a bullet (also known as the frozen rope), a lob (soft pass, usually over the heads of onrushing linemen), or something in between. The launch speed for a bullet is about 60 miles per hour, but the goal for all passes is to keep the ball in the air for as short a time as possible. The more time the ball is in the air, the more forces act on it—especially gravity and drag.

The quarterback's best friend is the tight spiral. The ball spins at roughly 600 revolutions per minute when thrown in a tight spiral, giving the ball greater speed for longer and, therefore, greater range. When the ball wobbles like a top winding down, the revolutions per minute slow down as well. That means the ball doesn't cut through the air as well and goes slower for a shorter distance. It tends to not go where the quarterback aimed it. Romo had to master the tight spiral, among many other things.

Lee told *New York Times* reporter Juliet Macur, "He [Romo] would get intercepted, and Bill Parcells would undress him. Man, he'd kill him and yell at him, but Tony wouldn't be fazed by it. He would come back and throw [a pass] that hit the guy right in the chest. I mean, what is it about this kid? You can't keep him down. You can't break his spirit."

Romo had a quality that is often called resilience. Where he got it, from his parents, his family, his faith, his genes, or his coaches and teammates or some combination, no one can say for sure. But it was noticeable: He had confidence even when he had failed. He coped and solved problems when they came up one by one. He accepted help and support and let bad feelings pass quickly.

MAKING THE TEAM

Partly because of his attitude and willingness to work, Romo made the Cowboys as the third quarterback for the 2003 preseason. He got his first chance in the NFL in a preseason game on August 9, 2003, against the Arizona Cardinals. On his very first play, he threw to rookie tight end Jason Witten for a 12-yard completion. He threw two more completions before throwing three incompletions and an interception. He ended up with four completions in eight passes and no touchdowns. No matter what happened from here, he had played in the NFL. No one could take that away.

Romo was then added to the Cowboys' roster, but on the practice squad (also called the "scout team"). Every NFL team can have 53 players and up to eight more on the practice squad. These practice players cannot play in regular season games but are invaluable in helping teams prepare for their next opponent. The quarterback of the scout team runs plays similar to those of the upcoming opponent. Romo was not satisfied just imitating other teams. Macur writes, "Romo soon became known for his ability to make something happen when the planned play breaks down." Defensive coaches can't prepare for plays that they haven't seen. Romo drove the Cowboys' defensive coaches crazy during practice.

His attitude was that he was serving an internship and he would somehow get promoted. He told Crouse, "That's all I kept thinking. Keep getting better."

The Cowboys had a 10–6 record in 2003, partly because their defense was one of the best in the NFL. Parcells knew defense, and he and his staff turned the team into a power-house that was hard to pass against and even harder to run against. But defense alone is usually not enough in the play-offs, and the Cowboys lost in the first round to the Carolina Panthers.

PRESEASON 2004: ALMOST GETTING CUT

As Cowboy rookies together, Romo and tight end Jason Witten had bonded. In the summer of 2004, Romo took time to help run the Burlington High School football camp. Soon it would become the Tony Romo All Position Football Camp and include several area coaches. Witten came with him and stayed in the Romos' basement. Romo returned the favor and went to Witten's football camp in Tennessee. Their friendship deepened.

Soon after Romo returned to Texas, he reported to training camp and found that he had an uphill battle to make the team for 2004. Suddenly, the Cowboys had too many quarterbacks.

Successful NFL teams must have good people at the four key levels of the organization: The owner, the general manager, the coach, and the quarterback all need to have ability and dedication for a team to have a chance at the ultimate prize, the Super Bowl. In early 2004, the Cowboys had everything but the quarterback. Quincy Carter was an experienced starter, and two other quarterbacks were brought in: Drew Henson and Vinny Testaverde. Henson looked like the model for an NFL quarterback. He was the son of a coach, scored a 39 on the Wonderlic (an impressive score), and was six foot four inches with a cannon for an arm. He was so good that he was the starting quarterback at the University of Michigan over Tom Brady, who went on to NFL stardom. Henson, however, had left the University of Michigan early because he wanted to play third base for the Yankees. He was having trouble hitting curveballs and was ready to come back to football. The Cowboys signed him to an eight-year contract.

Testaverde had been with Parcells when he coached the New York Jets, and he was very experienced. That meant that three quarterbacks—Carter, Testaverde, and Henson—were ahead of Romo on the depth chart going into the 2004 preseason. Teams never keep four quarterbacks. Romo was about to be the odd man out.

Then, the football world was shocked when Carter was suddenly cut on August 4, 2004, possibly for failing a drug test. Reports came out of the Cowboys' training camp that Carter had not liked the signing of Testaverde. Perhaps Parcells and Jerry Jones were also not ready and willing to let Romo go.

Nevertheless, Romo struggled in a preseason game on August 9, 2004, against the Texans in Houston. He threw two interceptions and was sacked twice, once for a Texan safety. He was so bad that, when his father met him outside the stadium after the game, Ramiro asked whether the Cowboys would allow Romo back on the team bus to Dallas. Rumors started to fly that the Cowboys were looking for another experienced quarterback to back up Testaverde.

THE GAME THAT MAY HAVE SAVED HIS CAREER

The Cowboys traveled to play the Oakland Raiders in their second 2004 preseason game on August 21. It was a hostile place to play. Writer Hunter Thompson noted that Raiders fans were "beyond doubt the sleaziest and rudest and most sinister mob of thugs and wackos ever assembled." And Thompson was a Raiders fan.

The Cowboys were losing 20-15 with about four minutes left in the game and the ball in their own territory. Parcells, who hated to lose any game, even preseason ones, put Romo in. Romo at first looked unsure and threw an interception, but the play was called back because of a defensive penalty. He then drove the team down the field and, with 23 seconds remaining, threw a 13-yard strike to tight end Sean Ryan, who was tackled on the one-yard line. There were no time-outs left. The coaches screamed for Romo to spike the ball and stop the clock.

Instead, Romo called a play: He would run a quarterback keeper—he would look as though he might pass and then keep the ball and run for the end zone. If it worked, he was going to be a hero. If it didn't, Lee later told Engel, Romo would probably have been cut that night. Romo took the snap, hesitated enough to make the defense scramble to cover the receivers, and headed for the end zone. He scored with almost no time left. That night, Romo won more than the game. He soon became an active member of the team, not the practice squad.

2004 REGULAR SEASON

The Cowboys opened the 2004 regular season in Minnesota against the Vikings. In the first quarter, Cowboy punter Mat McBriar fumbled a snap on a field goal try so Parcells put Romo in to hold the ball for field goals and extra points. He would become the holder for the rest of the season.

When Testaverde faltered and led the team to a 3–6 start, it was Henson, not Romo, who was called on next. Cowboys receiver Keyshawn Johnson told Engel that Romo was not yet ready in 2004: "He'd want to force the ball into tight situations. And that means you can be prone to turnovers. So on him, I was a yes, but no. I thought he could play if somebody didn't care about his gunslinger mentality."

On Thanksgiving Day against the Chicago Bears, Parcells started Henson. The team had paid a good deal of money for Henson, and owner Jerry Jones reportedly wanted to try Henson out and see what he had bought. The young quarterback looked lost. He threw an interception to Bears cornerback R.W. McQuarters, who returned it for a touchdown. Henson completed only 4 of his 12 passes for 31 yards. His quarterback rating was 7.6 (158.3 is the highest). Henson was put back on the bench for good by Parcells, who clearly thought he wasn't ready for prime time. Testaverde came in and led a fourth-quarter charge, and the Cowboys won the game.

The season was not a good one for the Cowboys. They ended in a three-way tie for last place in the National Football Conference (NFC) East division with a 6–10 record. Testaverde would not be brought back for the next season, but Romo always learns from those around him, and he had learned from the veteran. Engel reports:

> His biggest progress that season [in 2004] had been having his locker next to Testaverde all season. Both Romo and Parcells later credited that year of sitting

next to the veteran for teaching him how to study, prepare, and play—in effect, becoming franchise quarterback material.

Parcells had now seen more of Romo, and his criticisms had turned into more of an affectionate needling. The Dallas Cowboy Web site reported in 2004 that, after Romo had missed on several passes in practice, Parcells said, "I was telling him I bet his girlfriend probably didn't get many teddy bears when he took her to the arcade." *USA Today's* Tom Weir later wrote that,

THE NFL QUARTERBACK RATING SYSTEM

Almost every professional football fan agrees that the NFL quarterback rating system is hard to understand. Most quarterbacks do not know how to figure out their own rating. The system is so complicated, in fact, that it was the opening problem for a college algebra text on a difficult set of math equations known as quadratics.

Don Smith, an NFL Hall of Fame executive, designed the NFL quarterback rating system in 1973. He wanted to grade quarterbacks with a number similar to what students get in school. A 100 would be excellent, and a 66.7 would be average. So far, so good. In each of four categories, a quarterback would be given 0 if he was below average, 1 if he was average, and 2 if he was superior. The four categories are: pass completion percentage (C), yards per attempt (Y), touchdown percentage (T), and interception percentage (I).

Smith realized some performances were so good that they had to be greater than 2 so he fiddled with the equations and made 2.375 the highest, instead of 2. He was a statistician at after a bad pass, Parcells liked to tell Romo that he was like a golf ball in high grass: lost. Romo could do a perfect imitation of his coach saying just that.

GETTING CLOSER TO STARTING

Parcells had decided that he needed another experienced quarterback that he knew well. Therefore, before the 2005 preseason, he signed Drew Bledsoe. Bledsoe had played for Parcells as a New England Patriot and led the team to the 1996 Super Bowl. Henson and Romo would compete for the role of backup.

heart. His overall equation is Rating = C + Y + T + I divided by 6 and multiplied by 100. That meant that if a quarterback got a 2.375 in each of the four categories, he would have a 158.3 as a perfect score.

The rating rewards a quarterback throwing several short passes ending up with a touchdown pass over a quarterback who covers the same ground in one long touchdown pass. It also is famous for what it doesn't measure—it doesn't take into account winning and doesn't penalize a passer who is sacked.

The score works well enough for many. The best career passer rating is Steve Young at 96.8. The best season rating has been Peyton Manning's 2004 rating of 121.1. John Elway, however, only had a 79.9 career rating, even though he had more wins than anyone except Brett Favre. And Troy Aikman ended at 81.6, partly because he had a great runner named Emmitt Smith and didn't primarily throw short passes—he handed the ball to Smith.

Romo (*above*) dedicated his time to improving his game, and he learned a great deal from more experienced players like Vinny Testaverde. Although he was only a backup quarterback, he eventually gained the respect of his teammates and Coach Parcells.

Sporting News reporter Ryan Fagan described Romo's focus during the training camps:

> If he ever wanted to get on the field, he had to focus on beating out the guy in front of him. Every year, he'd go back to the basics with his throwing mechanics, examining what worked and what needed work,

driven by the thought that there always was a way to improve his release or strengthen his arm. He spent his time on footwork, dropping back and recognizing coverages. His attitude was, and still is, that he was going to work as hard as he could and let the chips fall where they may.

Romo told Fagan, "The people who are best under pressure are the ones who have done it a million times. That's what you try to do—throw five or six days a week and put yourself in a position where you've practiced that specific throw enough times."

In the early weeks of training camp in 2005, Romo told Engel, "You only get such a grace period in the NFL before you've got to produce." Romo got more playing time in the 2005 preseason because Parcells and Jones were ready to test him. Two years of studying and practicing had paid off. Romo did well in several 2005 preseason games. Parcells later told *USA Today* writer Tom Weir that he knew "we might have something" as Romo excelled in the preseason. He completed 23 of 37 passes for 237 yards and a touchdown. And he had avoided throwing an interception. Parcells told Weir, "Had he played his first or second year, he'd probably be out of football. With a player like Tony, who didn't really play big-time college football, he just needed time to get ready."

Deep down Parcells was still wanting to go with experience. Bledsoe did well enough to never let Romo see any real playing time all year. Romo, however, did make his first official NFL appearance as a quarterback in a regular season game on October 9, 2005. He went to one knee on the final drive of the game, a win over the Philadelphia Eagles.

In a crucial game in December at Giants Stadium in New Jersey, Bledsoe had not been able to rally the team against the Giants. Dallas lost the game 17-10, and the season became an immediate disappointment. The Cowboys had won more than they lost, going 9–7, but they missed the play-offs for the second straight year. For Jones and Parcells that was unacceptable. They soon made a move that would shake up the team and the football world.

Riding
the Ultimate
Roller-Coaster

On March 18, 2006, Jerry Jones took his private jet to Atlanta, Georgia, to pick up Terrell Owens and Owens's agent, Drew Rosenhaus. On the flight back to Dallas, they worked out the details of a three-year, $25 million contract for Owens, making him a Cowboys receiver.

Bill Parcells had some doubts, because Owens was famous for both his talent on the field and his ability to attract controversy off it. He had criticized both of his former quarterbacks, Jeff Garcia of the San Francisco 49ers and Donovan McNabb of the Philadelphia Eagles. He had famously said in 2005 that, if Brett Favre were the quarterback of the Eagles, and not McNabb, the Eagles would be undefeated. Not long after, Owens was deactivated by the Eagles.

Parcells had done some homework. He called many people he knew and asked, according to Mark Maske in *War Without Death*, "Does he respond to competition?" Parcells wanted to know if Owens really wanted to win or only pretended to. Some football fans considered Owens a narcissist, someone who always needs to be the center of attention. Some considered him an egotist, someone who thinks he is exceptional but can also prove it. A narcissist can destroy a team by demanding all the credit for success and none of the blame for failure. An egotist can help the team with extraordinary play even if he is obnoxious.

What made Owens extraordinary was his superb conditioning and his ability to make long runs after catching the ball. He was huge, fast, and at times unstoppable. But Owens expected and even demanded that the ball be thrown to him. Parcells had to warn him that the Cowboys did not have a "West Coast offense" (which uses many short passes) and so Owens would get fewer catches. Owens thought he could transform the offense.

TRAINING CAMP: THE FOURTH TIME IS THE CHARM

On July 29, 2006, the Cowboys opened up training camp at a resort in Oxnard, California—about an hour's drive north of Los Angeles. Jones liked to bring his team to California for training because it was cooler than the Cowboys' practice facility at Valley Ranch in Texas and because he knew the Cowboys had fans around the country.

A media center had been set up on a tennis court because many reporters would be coming to see Owens. While a band played live music and the sidelines filled with blow-up props for Tostitos, Miller Lite beer, and Ford Motors, more than 5,000 fans milled around to watch opening-day practice.

This was Romo's fourth training camp. Parcells and Jones had agreed that they needed to give Romo a chance at being

The controversial wide receiver Terrell Owens (*left*), joined the Dallas Cowboys in 2006. Owens may have been the center of attention at that year's preseason training camp, but Parcells (*right*) and his coaches were also focused on preparing Romo for game time.

their starter sometime this year if Drew Bledsoe didn't perform well. Parcells told *USA Today* writer Tom Weir that he was determined to "really go forward and try to get him [Romo] ready this preseason." Parcells could be seen wearing a long-sleeved shirt with a picture on the back: two hands pushing poker chips toward the middle of a table. The shirt read, "Who's All In?" This was a year when gambling and risk-taking were in the air.

During the first practice, Romo dropped back and threw a perfect touchdown pass to Owens. The fans cheered wildly, even more so when Owens raised his arms and urged them on. They began to chant Owens's initials, "T-O, T-O." After the practice they descended on Owens with anything they could lay their hands on for him to sign—footballs, jerseys, programs, hats, and more.

Owens got all the media attention, but the Cowboys had been smart enough to lock in another gifted receiver: Romo's best friend and roommate, tight end Jason Witten, was given a six-year, $29 million contract as training camp opened. And, one of Romo's main rivals for backup quarterback, Drew Henson, was released. Parcells was going all in on Romo as backup and perhaps as a starter soon.

2006 PRESEASON

Romo played the entire preseason opener against the Seattle Seahawks. He completed 19 of 25 passes for 235 yards and a touchdown. Parcells wanted him to get the feel of an entire game. He wanted to let him experience all of its ups and downs, the ebb and flow of luck and emotion and exhaustion. Writer Mac Engel reports that days later Parcells said that he needed "to coach him all the way through the game. You have to keep him right on it, keep him focused on it, keep reminding him of things." He sounded like a father talking about his son.

Romo played well in every preseason game. Parcells told Weir, "This preseason, what that allowed him to do is really get the feeling of responsibility, that he's not just going in to relieve somebody. A couple of games I said, 'You're playing it, don't plan on coming out.' That makes him say, 'OK, this is on me; nobody is bailing me out.'"

Romo was rewarded with a two-year, $3.9 million contract extension on August 31. He would make $2 million in a signing bonus, the same $900,000 salary he had been scheduled to make for 2006, and $1 million for 2007. The Cowboys clearly didn't want to lose him to another team, but the veteran Bledsoe was still the starting quarterback.

REGULAR SEASON PLAYING TIME

On October 15, 2006, Romo saw his first regular season NFL action other than holding the ball for kicks or kneeling at the end of a game. With the Cowboys leading the Houston Texans, he was brought in to get some playing time. His first official NFL regular game pass was to a rookie, Sam Hurd, who caught the ball for a 33-yard gain. The completion was also Hurd's first catch. Romo's next pass went to Owens, who scored a touchdown. Romo was 2 for 2, with a perfect quarterback rating of 158.3. His first taste of success and victory was sweet. The Cowboys won, 34-6. The next game would not be so easy.

ESPN heavily advertised its *Monday Night Football* game on October 23 between the division-rival Cowboys and Giants. The sports network received the highest ratings in cable television history for the game. Late in the second quarter, the Giants led 12-7. Bledsoe went back to pass, and Owens was open on the right side of the field. Instead of throwing there, Bledsoe threw to Terry Glenn on the left, who was not open. Giant Sam Madison intercepted the ball. On the sidelines, Parcells was furious. Something snapped. It was now time for Romo.

On the first play from scrimmage after halftime, Romo went back to pass. He threw to rookie tight end Anthony Fasano, but Giant superstar Michael Strahan deflected the ball and linebacker Antonio Pierce intercepted it. The Giants furiously rushed the new quarterback for the rest of the game, smelling blood. Romo threw two more interceptions, and one of them was returned for a touchdown.

Romo also threw a spectacular 53-yard touchdown pass to Patrick Crayton and another to Owens. For the game he completed 14 of 25 passes for 227 yards. It was enough to build on.

The Giants won, 36-22. Romo was disappointed with that result, but he had played well enough to win the starting job. Engel writes that Romo said after the game, "I don't feel very good about the situation right now. I definitely would have liked to have performed better. Hopefully next week that will change."

THE RISE BEGINS

Next week things did change. He was about to enter one of the most rapid rises and falls of a sports figure in recent history.

Romo's first start was on October 29 against the Carolina Panthers, and he was just short of brilliant. His second start was against the Washington Redskins on November 5, 2006. He played well and drove the team toward a tie-breaking score when he completed a crucial 28-yard pass to Witten at the Redskins' 17-yard line with six seconds remaining. But Redskin defensive back Troy Vincent blocked a field-goal try, and safety Sean Taylor scooped up the loose ball and ran it back into Cowboy territory. After a penalty, the Redskins kicked a 47-yard field goal to win, 22-19. It one of the strangest endings to any Redskins-Cowboys game in history, but Romo had completed 24 of 35 passes for 284 yards and two touchdowns. He was effective and had played well enough to win.

The next week, against the Arizona Cardinals, Romo could not be stopped. He passed for 308 yards and two touchdowns, completing 20 of 29 passes. His rating was 126.8. The Cowboys won 27-10. Moreover, he was named the NFC

Offensive Player of the Week. He became the first Cowboy quarterback to pass for more than 250 yards in three consecutive weeks since the legendary Troy Aikman had done it in 1993. Nine starting quarterbacks before Romo had failed to reach that milestone.

On November 19, the unbeaten Indianapolis Colts led by Peyton Manning came to play the Cowboys in Texas Stadium on a beautiful fall afternoon. Manning was the rival quarterback Romo had most studied on film and in person. This was a showdown between master and student. The master won the first half. But the game turned in the third quarter on a defensive play: Linebacker Kevin Burnett intercepted a Manning pass and ran it 39 yards into the end zone. The score was tied, 7-7.

Late in the fourth quarter, the Cowboys led 21-14. But no one-touchdown lead is safe against Manning. The Cowboys had a third-down-and-seven with 2:09 to play. The coaches called in a run play. After reading the defense, Romo changed it to a pass, hitting Terry Glenn for a seven-yard gain and a first down that kept Manning off the field. That simple change of play won the game.

Manning met up with Romo on the field after the game. He put his arm around him, and said, "You're a good player." Romo sprinted off the field with the game ball held high over his head, smiling broadly. Cowboys fans were getting to like that smile. *New York Times* reporter Karen Crouse spoke to Parcells and Owens after the game. She wrote:

> Parcells has said that the injection of Romo into the starting lineup has perked him up a little bit. The whole team seems to have benefited from the spotlight shifting from Terrell Owens's mouth to Romo's arm.
>
> "You have a leader of the team and he's out there having fun, it's just contagious," said Owens. . . . "It kind of rubs off on you."

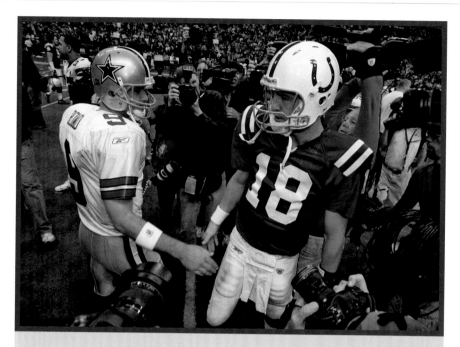

After several close games in the 2006 season, Romo's first as starting quarterback, the Cowboys won against the undefeated Indianapolis Colts. Peyton Manning (*right*), the Colts leader and one of the best quarterbacks in NFL history, complimented Romo (*left*) on his performance in the game.

THANKSGIVING DAY GALLOPING GOBBLER AWARD

Romo was now in a zone where the physical and mental work as one. His passes seemed effortless and unforced. He was making the right decisions about whom to throw to and when. His timing was almost perfect. He had taken the challenging and rewarding task of being a professional quarterback and made it look easy, at least for a few games. He was in a flow, like a baseball player on a hot hitting streak or a basketball player who can't be stopped.

On Thanksgiving Day, November 23, 2006, the Tampa Bay Buccaneers played the Cowboys at Texas Stadium in front of a national television audience. Romo came out throwing. He threw a 30-yard touchdown to Terry Glenn, and then a two-yarder, also to Glenn. He threw a touchdown to running back Marion Barber. At halftime, the Cowboys led 21-10.

Parcells took Romo aside in the locker room and said it was important to deliver a knockout punch early in the third quarter. Any NFL team can quickly come back from an 11-point deficit. Romo took the advice and threw a touchdown pass to Barber, and then another to Owens. The final score was 38-10. Romo had passed for five touchdowns and 306 yards. It was only the ninth time in club history that a quarterback threw five touchdown passes in a game, and the first since Aikman in 1999.

The news media swarmed around Romo at the end of the game. A Fox Sports employee had trouble giving Romo the Thanksgiving Galloping Gobbler Award because of all the reporters trying to interview him. Karen Crouse wrote that above Romo was a colorful handmade sign in the stands that said, "Give Thanks for Tony Romo."

The coach of the Bucs, Jon Gruden, told Crouse, "I thought it was Aikman out there. I think he is a very polished technician now." Parcells, though, wanted everyone to calm down. At the press conference after the game, he said, "I could have thrown those first two [touchdown passes]." Tom Weir reported that Parcells then gave Romo some homework:

> "I told him to Google up the name of a guy whose star burned real brightly for a short time in this league," says Parcells, declining to specify the flash in the pan. . . . Given that Parcells proudly describes himself as a Neanderthal, Romo says his reaction was, "You've worked on a computer before?"

Parcells was proud of Romo, and he liked that Romo was a student of football history. Weir reported that Romo kept a copy of *Johnny U: The Life and Times of John Unitas* (by Tom Callahan) in his locker. Unitas is considered by many to have been the greatest quarterback of all time. Parcells said to Weir, "That's one thing I like about Tony. He wants to know about his predecessors. A lot of good players that I have had have exhibited that characteristic."

JOHN UNITAS

John Constantine Unitas was born on May 7, 1933, in Pittsburgh, Pennsylvania. His father died when he was five, and his mother worked two jobs to support her family. Johnny (as he was called, although he didn't like the name) worked part time shoveling coal into cellars.

He didn't look like an athlete. He was thin, with slumping shoulders, and a loose-jointed walk. He was called goofy. He was so shy that he sat in the parking lot during school dances.

Like Tony Romo, he was not offered scholarships by any of the major football programs, so he went to the University of Louisville in Kentucky. Legend has it that he weighed 145 pounds (66 kg) on his first day of college practice. But he had a good college career and was drafted in the ninth round by the Steelers. He was cut, however, before the season began.

Unitas then worked construction in and around Pittsburgh and played semiprofessional football in his spare time, earning $6 per game on fields than often had almost as much glass as grass. Someone noticed him, and in 1956 he received an invitation to a Baltimore Colt tryout. He had to borrow gas money to get there. The Colts signed him.

When the starting quarterback broke his leg, Unitas replaced him. Two years later, on December 28, 1958, he led

Soon after, Romo was named NFC Player of the Month. In November he had completed 85 of 117 passes for 1,124 yards and nine touchdowns. His quarterback rating was 124.7. It was perhaps the best first five games by a quarterback in NFL history. Fame not only touched him, it now surrounded him. Todd Archer wrote in the *Dallas Morning News:* "He is touted as the

his team on a 13-play overtime drive that mixed remarkable lobs and bullet passes to beat the Giants 23-17 in Yankee Stadium in the NFL Championship Game. The stands rocked so much that the main television cable was disconnected, resulting in a blackout of a few minutes. The game is commonly called the greatest football game ever played. Writer Michael MacCambridge argues in *America's Game* that, from that moment on, football replaced baseball as America's favorite sport.

Few remember that Unitas worked for Bethlehem Steel in the off-season. Pro football players of his era did not make enough money to support themselves; almost all had off-season jobs as well.

He would win a second and third championship. For his long 17-year career, he passed for 40,239 yards, the first player ever to pass for more than 40,000 yards. From 1956 to 1960, he threw a touchdown pass in 47 consecutive games, an accomplishment many sports experts compare to baseball's Joe DiMaggio hitting in 56 consecutive games. Both records are considered unbreakable. Unitas gave his uniform to the Pro Football Hall of Fame, but he hung onto his famous high-top shoes. He said they were good for cutting grass.

story of the year in the NFL, and the Cowboys are trendy again. Almost daily, it seems, Romo leads off ESPN's *SportsCenter*."

REVENGE ON THE GIANTS

Romo then played in his most important game to that point. The New York Giants had soundly beaten the Cowboys just a few weeks before, in Dallas. The Cowboys now had to go to East Rutherford, New Jersey, into Giants Stadium at the Meadowlands to face New York again, on December 3, 2006. The Meadowlands can spook a team. Legend has it that the Giants open doorways in stadium tunnels to create drafts that affect opponent's field goals and long passes. The wind howls in the stadium in a bone-chilling way, as do the fans.

The game was a tough, back-and-forth fight. The Cowboys led 20-13 in the fourth quarter, but Giant quarterback Eli Manning, the younger brother of Peyton, showed the flashes of brilliance that would earn him and his team a Super Bowl ring the next year. This crucial game was the first between the two young quarterbacks.

As Manning drove the Giants for a tying touchdown late in the game, Romo turned to offensive coordinator Todd Haley and famously said, "Let 'em score. Give me one minute with two time-outs, and we'll win." Romo ran onto the field with exactly one minute to go in regulation and two time-outs. The ball was on the Cowboys' 32-yard line. In many cases, a team will play for overtime and just run out the clock. It is too dangerous to take chances that deep in one's own territory that late in the game.

Romo didn't see it that way. Engel writes that in the huddle he told center Andre Gurode that he was going to scramble. That meant the lineman had to block for him longer. Romo then turned to Witten and said, "I'm going to go to my left, and I'm going to throw it on the inside over your right shoulder." The ball was snapped, Romo dodged the onrushing tacklers, went to his left, and launched a long throw to Witten. It was a perfect strike, to the inside of the field, over Witten's right shoulder. The play went 42 yards and set up the winning field goal with one second left. The final score was 23-20. The game was considered an instant classic.

Based on his remarkable play, Romo was soon named to the football all-star game, the Pro Bowl, to be played in February 2007. It was remarkable for a rookie quarterback to be honored that way. He was the first Cowboy quarterback to make the Pro Bowl since Aikman had done so 11 years earlier.

FALLING BACK TO EARTH

Romo had made mistakes in the Giants game. Parcells gave a warning at a press conference, reported by Karen Crouse: "So far he's been dodging bullets. They're flying at him. They just haven't hit him." Suddenly, the bullets started hitting.

The same man who helped bring Romo to the NFL helped start the worst fall of his young career. Sean Payton, former Cowboys offensive coordinator, was now the head coach of the New Orleans Saints. He knew Romo's habits well, and knowledge is power. On December 10, in a nationally televised Sunday night game at Texas Stadium, Payton showed the power he had over Romo and the Cowboys. He helped design a defense that trapped Romo in a small pocket, disrupted his vision of the field, and didn't allow him or his receivers to get free for long. Saints quarterback Drew Brees threw five touchdown passes against the Cowboys, partly because Payton knew which Cowboys had which weaknesses on defense, and Brees took advantage of that. The final score was 42-17.

According to Maske, Parcells told his players after the game that "football is a humbling game. This can happen to you at any time." Parcells feared that Romo had been overloaded with more and more offensive plays to master. What made matters worse was that word spread around the NFL that there was now a rough blueprint on how to handle Romo: Trap him, don't let him get outside the pocket to make big plays, and jump into his line of vision whenever possible.

TWO COSTLY LATE-SEASON LOSSES

The Cowboys were ready to play for the NFC East division lead when the Philadelphia Eagles came to Texas Stadium on Christmas Day. Celebrity watchers saw *American Idol* star Carrie Underwood in Jerry Jones's suite, a guest of her new boyfriend, Tony Romo. Underwood had rocketed to instant fame in 2005 by winning the popular television competition. She and Romo made a dazzling couple. Both knew what it was like to have the world suddenly pay attention to their every move.

The blueprint on how to stop Romo was in good hands with Eagles head coach Andy Reid and his staff. The Eagles dominated the game. They contained Romo by blitzing him from many directions. Instead of second-half heroics, Romo was sacked twice and threw two interceptions. The Eagles ran over the Cowboys' defense for 204 rushing yards. The Cowboys lost, 23-7. Romo suddenly looked like a rookie.

Perhaps the most humbling loss of all took place the following week, on New Year's Eve, at home against the 2–13 Detroit Lions. The final score was 39-31. Romo seemed to be having trouble holding onto the football, fumbling twice. He had fumbled seven times and thrown eight interceptions in the past five games. Even more alarming, he had been sacked 13 times in those games. Defenses were flying at him from everywhere. All of a sudden, his rapid rise was mirrored by a rapid fall.

Romo told *New York Times* reporter Tom Spousta, "People always want to point to reasons why a team or a guy isn't playing as well. The reality of it is that some weeks, teams do a good job and play well against you. They get a good rush." Ever since the New Orleans game, teams had played well against him. They knew that, if they limited his chances to scramble for big plays, they could neutralize his biggest strength. He was no longer a golden boy shining brightly.

NFL teams adapt very quickly to changing conditions. Romo was a change, and they had adapted. He would now need to adapt to their adaptations.

The Cowboys 9–7 record was good enough to get them into the 2006 play-offs as a wild card. In early January 2007, Parcells took Romo aside at the Cowboy Center at Valley Ranch as they prepared for the postseason. Maske reports that Parcells had a different diagnosis of Romo's problems other than the fact that teams were learning how to contain the new quarterback:

> "Did I tell you this was going to happen or not?" Parcells said to his quarterback.
>
> "Yeah," Romo said.
>
> Parcells didn't want to discourage Romo's creativity. It had produced more good than bad. But Parcells thought Romo suffered from overconfidence. Romo believed he could make the next-to-impossible play and that led to unnecessary risks, which led to mistakes.
>
> "You have to be aware in doing that sometimes you can do more damage than good," Parcells told Romo.

Romo had proven he was human. Most people lack confidence as beginners, then become more confident in themselves with experience. Some then become overconfident, convinced that they can do anything.

THE BIG STAGE

On January 6, 2007, the Cowboys arrived in Seattle, Washington, at Qwest Field to play the Seattle Seahawks as part of Wild-card Weekend. In his first postseason game, Romo looked confident, but not overconfident. He was in charge as he drove his team 78 yards and hit Patrick Crayton with a precise 13-yard touchdown pass with just a few seconds to go in the first half. The Cowboys led 10-6. Their defense was playing well since their offense was giving them time to rest.

The second half was filled with strange, game-changing plays. Cowboys rookie Miles Austin ran back a kickoff 93 yards for a touchdown. Then Cowboys receiver Terry Glenn lost a fumble in his own end zone for a safety that was first called a Seahawk touchdown and then overruled. The play inspired the Seahawks to go on a long scoring drive. With 4:18 remaining in the game, the Seahawks led 21-20.

Romo then orchestrated a brilliant drive: an 11-yard pass to Crayton, a 12-yard pass to Owens, a run by Julius Jones. With less than two minutes to go, Romo hit Witten with a clutch pass on what appeared to be a first down at Seattle's one-yard line. After a replay, the play was ruled to be a fourth down on the two-yard line. With 1:19 left to play, Romo stayed on the field to hold for a short field goal try by kicker Martín Gramática. This kick would be shorter than an extra point, and Gramática had made 204 of 206 extra point tries in his long career.

THE BOBBLE

What happened next lives on in NFL play-off history as "the Bobble." Romo tried to do what he had done countless times in the last three years: catch the snap from the center, place the ball upright on the ground, spin it so the laces faced away from the kicker, and slightly tilt the tip toward the kicker. The snap, catch, spin, and tilt is harder than it looks and requires precision.

Instead, Romo caught the ball but bobbled it as he tried to place it upright. He couldn't get a good grip in time for Gramática to kick it. But he kept his cool and almost made a spectacular play: He immediately picked up the ball and sprinted to his left, heading toward the corner of the Seahawk end zone. Romo would have been a hero if anyone had blocked Seahawk safety Jordan Babineaux. No one did. Romo was tackled from behind by the safety inches away from the

In the 2006 NFC Wild-card play-off, the Cowboys trailed the Seattle Seahawks by one point with less than two minutes left in the game. Romo bobbled the snapped ball as kicker Martin Gramática (*standing*) stepped in for a field goal attempt.

first down and a little more than a yard away from a winning touchdown.

Romo was stunned. He sat on the goal line clutching his face mask with both hands, then came to the sidelines and stared down. Blood was pouring from his left hand, an injury never explained. He would get one more desperation pass as the game ended, but it would fall incomplete in the end zone.

At the postgame press conference, Romo told reporters: "I don't know if I have ever felt this low at any point." He was in tears. He had let down his team and his coach. He didn't offer any excuses, even though commentator Troy Aikman would later point out that Romo had fallen victim to the "k-ball." The kicking ball—called the "k-ball"—was always new and usually shiny and slippery with the original waxy coat. Unlike the ball used for the rest of the plays, it was not broken in. For that reason, most teams have a special holder who is not the starting quarterback, who has become used to the throwing ball. The Cowboys were an exception. Months later, league policy would change, essentially requiring k-balls to be broken in so they would be easier to grip. It would be called the "Romo Rule."

In the locker room, silence descended on the team until Parcells spoke. Maske writes that the head coach said, "You are a great bunch of guys. I wish you great success. You'll do well no matter what I do, whether I come back or not."

On the team bus to the airport, very few spoke. On the plane trip home, some players and coaches tried to reassure Romo. Engel writes that quarterback coach David Lee said, "We're not here if it's not for you and what you did." As sports legend has it, those were the same words that baseball great Jackie Robinson said to his pitcher, Ralph Branca, after Branca had given up the most famous home run in baseball history to New York Giant Bobby Thomson in a 1951 play-off game against the Brooklyn Dodgers.

GETTING OVER THE BOBBLE

Juliet Macur reports that Romo moped on the couch for the next two weeks. Owens called him nearly every night and tried to cheer him up. His parents, sisters, friends, and teammates finally rallied him. In *Tony Romo,* Chuck Bednar reported that older sister Danielle was especially vocal in seeing to it that her brother moved past the Bobble. Like a character in a Greek tragedy, he now had a little more humility to go with his warrior pride.

The best way to forget was to play again, and the 2006 season wasn't quite over for Romo. He played in his first Pro Bowl in Hawaii on February 10. He replaced Marc Bulger in the second half and rallied the NFC to a tie with a touchdown pass to Cardinals receiver Anquan Boldin and a two-point conversion to Panther Steve Smith. The AFC later won, 31-28, but Romo had done well in his first all-star game. He threw for 156 yards, completing 11 of 19 passes. The humiliation of the Bobble would slowly lose some of its sting.

How would he respond to the Bobble when the next season started? Bednar wrote that "there was much debate among football fans and media pundits about Tony's future. . . . Would he rebound, or would he be one of those athletes who encounter adversity and fold?" Romo would soon answer that question.

The turbulent 2006 season had started with Romo as a backup and ended with him as one of the most famous players in the NFL. He had experienced a roller-coaster of emotions in the last five months, highs and lows more extreme than what most people experience in a lifetime. And the ride was just beginning.

Thrown into
Riches and Fame

Tony Romo didn't try to hide in the weeks and months after the Bobble. He accepted responsibility for the mistake publicly and often. He didn't try to blame others or the slippery k-ball. His popularity seemed to grow because of his shouldering of the blame.

He was, however, the butt of many jokes. Jay Leno said on the *Tonight Show* that Romo could get an endorsement deal from the maker of the candy bar Butterfinger. Bobble-head dolls named "Romo" appeared on eBay. Fans blogged that he must have had some styling mousse left on his fingers.

Living unashamedly, openly, and with good humor was his revenge. He appeared in a commercial for AT&T handling a television remote control without bobbling it. He threw out the first pitch at a Cubs-White Sox game. He was spotted at the Key Club on the Sunset Strip in Los Angeles singing one of his favorite songs, Journey's "Don't Stop Believin'" with the band Metal Skool. The YouTube video of it went viral. He flew to Nashville, Tennessee, to celebrate Carrie Underwood's twenty-fourth birthday with her, and she flew to Dallas to celebrate his twenty-seventh. He was her date at the Country Music Awards in Las Vegas. He judged the Miss Universe pageant in Mexico City in late May. He seemed to be enjoying his new celebrity status.

He also went back to one of his favorite pastimes, playing golf. Romo tried to qualify for the U.S. Open in early May. He shot an even-par 72 in the local tournament but missed the cut in the sectional round in Irving, Texas, when he shot one over par and didn't make the top 10. He also played in the American Century Celebrity Golf Championship in Lake Tahoe, one of the most beautiful courses in the country with mountains and the lake as a backdrop. Michael Jordan, John Elway, Kevin Costner, and Charles Barkley were just a few of the celebrities playing.

Fame had moved in with Romo. Fans now knew his favorite actor was Christian Bale and his favorite TV show was *24*. He told reporters he couldn't name a favorite actress because there were so many. His golf heroes were Jack Nicklaus, Tiger Woods, and Steve Stricker. He loved karaoke, even though he was not a natural singer.

Romo seemed to be handling his celebrity status well. He told *Sporting News* reporter Ryan Fagan, "It's still a little different to me sometimes because I'm still the same guy I was a few years ago." His father would later tell Juliet Macur, "Money and becoming a celebrity come with his job, but I know Tony realizes that your relationship with other people, especially your family, is the most important thing in life." He said that when his son comes home, he is the same old Tony.

After the Cowboys' season ended with the Bobble, Romo occupied himself with endorsement deals and publicity events. He returned to playing golf, one of his favorite sports, and unsuccessfully tried to qualify for the U.S. Open.

2007 TRAINING CAMP AND PRESEASON

The Cowboys' 2007 training camp began in the Alamodome in beautiful and historic San Antonio, Texas. Camp opened with a new head coach, Wade Phillips. Parcells had resigned two weeks after the heartbreaking play-off loss. Phillips had been named on February 8 as Parcells's replacement. A new offensive coordinator, Jason Garrett, would be working with Romo.

Cowboy fans showed Romo support during training camp. When he trotted off the practice field one day in early August 2007, he was met by swarms of fans who reached out for autographs with jerseys, footballs, and even a baby in a Cowboys outfit. Many spectators were wearing his No. 9 jersey, among the most popular items of NFL clothing sold online. His grandparents were in the stands watching as well, always wanting to be a part of his life. They were pleased that so many people cared about their grandson.

Reporter Ryan Fagan noted that Romo's training camp this time was very different from the previous year:

> He's the starter and his entire thought process has changed. Now, it's team, team, team. He talks with the offensive linemen and learns the motivations and thought processes behind why they do what they do. He jokes with Terrell Owens and helps the team's young receivers work on their routes. . . . He has learned to be receptive when other players have suggestions. Building those give-and-take relationships is part of the job, part of his maturation as a team leader.

He was growing into the job and adjusting to all the changes. After a mediocre preseason of two wins and two losses, however, the Cowboys' organization was anxious to see how Romo would respond in the regular season. The first game was a real challenge.

TAKING ON THE GIANTS IN WEEK ONE

The *Sunday Night Football* broadcasting crew arrived in Dallas on September 9 for the biggest 2007 season-opening game in the NFL. The Cowboys and Romo were a compelling story, as were the New York Giants and Eli Manning. The game was billed as Manning versus Romo, round 2. The two best young quarterbacks in the game stepped into the ring.

Romo soon answered the question about whether he would rebound from the terrible play-off loss. In the Cowboys' first possession, Romo led them on a 14-play drive that ended in a field goal. He then threw a 12-yard touchdown pass to Witten in the second quarter and another to Owens in the third quarter. He even ran for his first career touchdown.

Manning kept pace as well. The Giants were picking apart the Cowboy defense. Late in the fourth quarter with the score 38-35 in favor of the Cowboys, the Giants prepared to send a safety to blitz Romo and disrupt him. That, after all, was part of the blueprint to beat him that teams knew from the previous year: Bring blitzers from everywhere, disrupt his vision, keep him in a small pocket, and confuse him.

Romo was not confused. He had adjusted to the league's blueprint to defeat him. He anticipated the blitz and told receiver Sam Hurd to watch for it and slip into the spot left by the safety. The ball was snapped, and Romo threw a perfect pass to Hurd where the safety should have been. Hurd scored a touchdown that sealed the game. The Cowboys won 45-35, and Romo had his best day as a pro with 345 yards, four touchdown passes, and one touchdown run. His quarterback rating was 128.5. Any questions about whether his confidence was hurt from the previous season were answered. He, not Manning, was named the NFC Offensive Player of the Week.

TEARING UP THE LEAGUE

In Week 2, the Miami Dolphins couldn't stop Romo and the Cowboys, who won 37-20. On one play, Dolphin linebacker

When Romo arrived at the Cowboys 2007 training camp in San Antonio, Texas, eager fans greeted him with requests for autographs and pictures. After his 2006 season, Romo was expected to improve his performance and lead his team under a set of new coaches.

Joey Porter had Romo in his grasp as other Dolphins converged on Romo for a sack. Somehow, Romo got the ball out to his tight end Tony Curtis, who later told reporters, "I didn't know how he could. I didn't think I was open. I'm the third option on that play." In *Tony Romo,* Mac Engel wrote that, during a time-out late in the game, a song used to introduce wrestler Hulk Hogan blared over the loudspeakers. Romo sang along, and some of the Dolphins stared at him. His teammate Anthony Fasano later said, "This is how he is. He sings Vanilla Ice, all of that stuff during the game. At the top of his lungs."

The fourth game of the 2007 season, on September 30 at Texas Stadium against the St. Louis Rams, is remembered for one play. At midfield, Romo lined up in the shotgun (the quarterback receives the ball five to seven yards back from the center rather than standing over the center). Center Andre Gurode hiked the ball well over Romo's head. The race for the loose ball was on, between Romo and several Rams players. The quarterback finally grabbed the bouncing ball at his own 16-yard line and now had to escape at least five tacklers. He ran by two defenders, faked a pass to fool two others, somehow avoided another tackler, and ran up the left sideline before running out of bounds at the Ram 46-yard line. He gained four yards, but had run more than 70 through a minefield of Rams. Fox play-by-play announcer Joe Buck simply called it "unbelievable . . . the legend just grew." Cowboys coach Wade Phillips told reporters, "It was a miracle play," and it reminded him of the legendary Roger Staubach, who had been similarly able to avoid and baffle tacklers with fakes and changes of speed and direction. That one play may have demoralized the Rams. The Cowboys won 35-7, and Romo ended up passing for 339 yards and three touchdowns while running for a fourth.

A STRANGE NIGHT IN BUFFALO

The Cowboys were now 4–0 in 2007 and the talk of the NFL, along with the unbeaten New England Patriots. Romo had not only survived his disaster during the 2006 play-offs in Seattle, but he had also become one of the most feared quarterbacks in the league. He was named NFL Offensive Player of the Month, completing 72 of 121 passes in September for 1,199 yards, eleven touchdowns, and only three interceptions. His rating was 112.9, second only to the Patriots' Tom Brady, who was also having a great season.

The Cowboys' next game, in Buffalo on October 8, was to be played on *Monday Night Football*. The Bills' coach, Dick Jauron, was a particularly intelligent designer of defenses. He knew that the blueprint to stop Romo needed some updating. He designed several blitzes that Romo would not be able to read. The Bills rushed Romo from everywhere, violently and relentlessly. They probed for weaknesses in his pass protection and found them. They clawed at the ball.

Twice in the first half, the Bills returned interceptions for touchdowns. By the last quarter, Romo had thrown five interceptions. Announcers Tony Kornheiser and Ron Jaworski were talking about the embarrassment Romo must be feeling in front of a national audience. The Cowboys trailed 24-13 going into the fourth quarter.

Romo kept throwing. Amazingly, he led the Cowboys on three scoring drives in the fourth quarter. The first scoring drive led to a field goal. Then, Romo hit Patrick Crayton with a four-yard touchdown pass with 20 seconds left. The Cowboys recovered an onside kick. Romo completed two more passes and rookie Nick Folk kicked a field goal with no time left for the Cowboys to win, 25-24.

Writer Sal Paolantonio, in *How Football Explains America*, set the scene after the game:

> Romo—his face and arms bloodied and battered— stood in the corner of the locker room, swallowing a slice of pizza, watching highlights of his Houdini act on *SportsCenter*, like he was a 15-year-old hanging out in his buddy's basement after the game.
>
> "I just told the guys in the huddle that we were going to come back and win this thing," he said.
>
> Said tight end Jason Witten, as he got dressed to board the team bus back to the airport, . . . "In the huddle, Tony was calm as could be. Nothing gets to him. He took charge in that huddle at the beginning of the fourth quarter, and that's how we came back and won."

Troy Aikman told Paolantonio that taking command of the huddle is crucial for a quarterback: "Sometimes you don't have to say a thing. The other players can tell just by looking in your eyes." Romo had always been able to project leadership in the huddle. Nowhere was that more evident than that long night in Buffalo. After the game, offensive coordinator Garrett told Juliet Macur, "I don't know why Tony is as resilient as he is, but I do know that's the mark of a great competitor. The Michael Jordans, the Tiger Woodses, guys like that all have that trait. . . . They have this tremendous belief in themselves."

PERSONAL LIFE MADE PUBLIC

It was around this time that Romo got a shock—his father had prostate cancer. Suddenly, the thrills of victory and agonies of defeat didn't seem as important. Ramiro, though, was lucky. The cancer had been detected relatively early, and he also had many people around him for support. Joan, now 50, was strong and capable and would help her husband through this crisis. Romo's sister Jossalyn, now 29, was a nursing student and could help. Danielle, 31, was a teacher and would also be part of the family support group. Father and son made plans to spend even more time together after the season.

The blow to the family from Ramiro's illness was softened by a financial windfall. On October 30, 2007, in a press room in Irving, Texas, filled with cameras and media, Romo signed a contract extension that gave him financial security. The contract was for a total of $67.5 million over six years. Ramiro and Joan sat in the audience and beamed with pride.

The contract guaranteed $30 million. Unlike players in virtually every other professional sport, football players are not guaranteed much of their salary if they are injured or perform badly. A signing bonus of $11.5 million as part of the $30 million guarantee meant that Romo would not have to worry about money for the rest of his life if he and his advisers managed his finances well.

At the press conference, reported by Todd Archer of the *Dallas Morning News,* owner Jerry Jones spoke fondly of Romo: "This is a feel-good story sitting here today. In many ways, it's about an individual that just wouldn't take no for an answer." Romo said, "I don't think I've made it. . . . The next

AIKMAN AND STAUBACH: TWO QUARTERBACK STYLES

Tony Romo stepped into a tradition of great Cowboys quarterbacks that includes Roger Staubach and Troy Aikman. The two represent two different styles of quarterbacking. Staubach was known as "Roger the Dodger" because of his ability to run and make tacklers miss. He often played best when a play had broken down and he had to improvise. He was a gambler. Aikman, on the other hand, stayed in the pocket; when a play broke down, he often simply threw the ball out of bounds and moved on to the next play. He was not a gambler—he liked things to be precise and predictable.

One type of quarterback is often called a renegade, a gunslinger, or a maverick. Staubach, Brett Favre, John Elway, Donovan McNabb, and Tony Romo are examples. The other type is often called a systems guy or a game manager. Troy Aikman, Tom Brady, John Unitas, Peyton Manning, and Drew Brees are examples. The fact that the gunslingers named above have five Super Bowl rings and the managers have 11 rings leads many organizations to prefer the managers over the gunslingers. But both can win.

Of course, all quarterbacks have at least some of both styles. And what both types of quarterbacks have in common is that they keep their heads while others around them are losing theirs. At a key moment near the end of Super Bowl XXIII, Joe Montana sensed that his team was tense and anxious. As he stood in the huddle, he pointed out that comedian and actor John Candy was in the stands. His team relaxed and made crucial plays to win the game.

step is always on the field. I don't think this in any way changes that." The contract was not something he had fought for out of greed or the need to make more than other quarterbacks. It was a reward given to him. And he shared the reward, giving $100,000 to Eastern Illinois University.

AMERICA'S MOST ELIGIBLE CELEBRITY BACHELOR

He was now famous and rich at the age of 27. The world knew his familiar smile, his love for life and sports, and his offbeat antics. He was one of America's most eligible bachelors, falling into and out of relationships with several stars. He had broken up with Carrie Underwood, telling her that he needed to devote more time to football. But he had found other dates, including singer Britney Spears. *People.com* reported on October 25, 2007, that *One Tree Hill* star Sophia Bush enjoyed Romo's company on several dates, including one at the popular N9NE Steakhouse in Dallas, with several other Cowboys and their wives and girlfriends. Bush and Romo were also at a party at Terence Newman's house, previewing the video game *Guitar Hero III*. Bush enjoyed watching Romo's competitive streak come alive in an area other than football; *People.com* reported that they laughed their way through the party.

Famous people tend to meet other famous people and feel comfortable around one another. They know what it feels like to be suddenly pursued by fans and the media. They know the hidden cost of fame—the loss of privacy. Soon after he signed his contract, the tabloids were filled with rumors about a new girlfriend—singer and actress Jessica Simpson. Their relationship became a subject for football fans, celebrity watchers, and anyone else who followed the news. Romo now had a celebrity status only a few NFL players achieve. Unlike many famous athletes, he welcomed becoming a celebrity, someone famous for being famous. He was no longer known just for what he did on the football field.

Fame comes through achievement. Celebrity comes through personality. They are different, but the combination is potent. A

In 2007, Romo signed a contract extension with the Dallas Cowboys, receiving $67.5 million dollars over a period of six years. Cowboys owner Jerry Jones (*right*) announced the extension to the press with Romo by his side.

celebrity tends to become a character that people want to talk about. And Romo was now a true celebrity.

COMPLETING A DREAM SEASON

By mid-October 2007, the Cowboys were 5–0 for the first time in 24 years. Romo had started 15 games and had an 11–4 record. He had been by turns brilliant and mistake-prone, but the bottom line was that he was a winner and the Cowboys leader for the near future at least.

The Cowboys met their match. On October 14, the New England Patriots came to Texas Stadium. It was a rare clash of 5–0 teams and advertised as a dramatic showdown between the two highest-rated quarterbacks in the league, Romo and Tom Brady.

The game was close for more than a half, with the Cowboys leading 24-21 in the third quarter. Brady, however, took his game to another level: He threw five touchdown passes. These Patriots had receivers Randy Moss, Wes Welker, and Donté Stallworth, and a host of other offensive weapons. The Cowboys couldn't stop them in the fourth quarter, and the Patriots won 48-27. Romo had been good, completing 18 of 29 for two touchdowns. Brady had been better than good. The Patriots would go on to an undefeated regular season and be considered one of the best teams of all time. The Cowboys now knew they still had some work to do. Romo had lost an important battle for league supremacy at quarterback.

Nonetheless, few teams could beat the 2007 Cowboys. On November 11, they went to the Meadowlands and soundly beat their NFC East rival the New York Giants. On the first drive, the Giants' pass rush closed in on Romo, but he scrambled out of the pocket and found tight end Tony Curtis along the left sideline. *New York Times* reporter Judy Battista wrote: "It is in those moments that Romo seems to sparkle the most, when he escapes the pocket and sees the entire field open up. He fired a pass to Curtis, who by then was alone in the back corner of the end zone. It was precisely what the Giants . . . did not want Romo to do." The Cowboys won the crucial game 31-20.

The team went on to a remarkable 13–3 season and won the NFC East division title. Romo's regular season statistics set three Cowboy single-season records: He completed 335 passes for 4,211 yards and 36 touchdown passes.

The regular season was slightly marred by a late-season loss to the Eagles, 10-6. A few days later, Owens joked that Jessica Simpson might be taking Romo's focus away from the game. Some Cowboy fans didn't take it as a joke, and injuries had taken their toll on the team. Romo was playing with a damaged thumb on his throwing hand, and Owens had a severe ankle sprain.

WEEKEND IN CABO

Wade Phillips gave his players three days off after the regular season to relax before their play-off game with the New York Giants. Romo and Simpson went to the resort area Los Cabos (containing the town Cabo San Lucas, just called "Cabo"), at the southern tip of the Baja California peninsula in Mexico. They rented a house with Jason Witten, Terence Newman, and others and relaxed and partied in a paradise with views of spectacular blue-green water set against steep hillsides. Romo later said it was nice to not have to worry about answering his phone or doing radio or television shows for a few days.

The price of being a celebrity, however, hit Romo hard. Many Cowboys fans and pundits in the media turned the get-away into a tale of overconfidence and a lack of seriousness about beating the Giants. Photos showing Romo, Simpson, Witten, and others relaxing by a pool became locker-room material the Giants could use to motivate themselves. *New York Times* reporter William C. Rhoden said Romo had just kicked sand in the Giants' face.

The story became so big that some began to wonder why it provoked such a deep response. The biblical tale of Samson and Delilah—of a strong man weakened by love—was mentioned on at least one talk show. Theories on why a larger society frowns on two lovers escaping responsibility in a worldly paradise suddenly appeared. In response, Romo told *New York Times* reporter John Branch, "I just live my life. I try to work hard at football. I try to do things the right way."

SHOWDOWN WITH THE GIANTS IN THE PLAY-OFFS

For Romo's second play-off game and first divisional championship game, the stakes were higher than ever. On January 13, 2008, the Giants and Cowboys faced off for the third time that season. Like Romo's first play-off game, it was close, tense, and filled with odd plays on both sides.

The Cowboys' game plan seemed to be to run the ball. Marion Barber had run for 101 yards by halftime, and the Cowboys were playing conservatively. The Giants' game plan seemed to include harassing the Cowboys' offensive line with a vicious pass rush to keep Romo in check.

A 15-yard penalty on the Cowboys helped the Giants to score just before halftime, making it 14-14. Romo led a long drive that took more than half of the third quarter, but a dropped pass and penalties meant that the Cowboys only scored a field goal. A long punt return by R.W. McQuarters led to a go-ahead touchdown for the Giants, 21-17.

With 1:50 left, the Cowboys needed to go 48 yards to win. In similar situations, Romo had performed magic time and again. He completed a remarkable scrambling shovel pass to Witten that got the Cowboys to the Giants' 22-yard line with 31 seconds left. But a penalty and a mistake in the end zone—Patrick Crayton and Romo seemed to have two different pass routes in mind—led to a McQuarters interception, and suddenly the game and the 2007 season were over for the Cowboys.

The loss hit the Cowboys and Romo hard. Many fans and people in the media blamed the trip to Cabo, but the fact is that the Giants won the game the same way they would beat the undefeated New England Patriots in the Super Bowl a few weeks later: a great pass rush, miraculous Manning passes, and a grinding running game.

The season wasn't over yet for Romo. He had only started 26 games in the NFL, but he was invited to his second Pro Bowl, which he started on February 10, 2008. He completed 9 of 16 passes for 87 yards and two touchdowns. One was caught by Arizona Cardinals' wide receiver Larry Fitzgerald, who would play brilliantly during the Cardinals' Super Bowl run the next season. The other was to Terrell Owens. The NFC won, 42-30.

Romo now had to face an off-season filled not with questions about the Bobble but ones about Cabo. His resiliency would be tested again.

An Elite Quarterback

The off-season was once again filled with the pleasures and duties that come with being a super-celebrity. In January 2008 Victoria's Secret compiled its annual list of the "Sexiest Male Athletes," and that year Romo took over the top spot from Tom Brady. In New York City at *Cosmopolitan* magazine's Fun Fearless Male awards, Romo was honored along with many other male celebrities. Two of them had also dated Jessica Simpson—Dane Cook and John Mayer—leading Romo to joke to the Associated Press that dating Simpson was one of the qualifications for the award. He said that playing football also made him fearless.

CELEBRITY POWER COUPLE

By 2008, the Romo-Simpson relationship had become world-famous. And ever since the loss to the Giants, some Cowboys fans had pinned part of the blame on Simpson. *Texas Monthly* writer Gary Cartwright told Rich Cohen of *Vanity Fair:* "The greatest quarterbacks are 100 percent dedicated to the game. But Romo seems happy-go-lucky. If they win, he seems happy. If they lose, he seems happy. And all this is tied up with Jessica Simpson."

Simpson told Cohen: "Dating the Cowboys quarterback comes with hype, the fans, the bloggers, but I've never dated a guy that was more simple. I'm always there for him after the game, and he knows he has me to come home to." She told *Glamour* magazine that Romo "reintroduced me to myself. . . . He made me feel comfortable again."

When Romo and Simpson went to Burlington in June 2008, he entered a golf tournament in Riverside, Wisconsin, along with his father. The younger Romo shot a three-under-par 69. While he was playing, Simpson had lunch with Joan Romo in Madison at Marsh Shapiro's Nitty Gritty. *Madison.com* writer Doug Moe reported that a girls' basketball team from Illinois happened to be there for lunch as well, and someone from the team got up the courage to ask Simpson if she could take a picture with her. "Absolutely," Simpson said. The restaurant owner then described what happened: "She slid out of her booth and . . . was mobbed. She was signing their uniforms, and everyone was either taking pictures with their cell phones or calling back to Illinois and screaming that they were having lunch . . . with Jessica Simpson."

The Romo-Simpson relationship had many ups and downs, and it probably ended in July 2009. Yet they had helped each other get through difficult but exciting parts of their young lives. They lived in the spotlight and received harsh criticism, but both were capable of sacrifices to the relationship and to each other.

GETTING BACK TO FOOTBALL

The NFL season really begins in the off-season. Organized team activities (OTAs) are off-season practices—teams are

Romo's high-profile relationship with celebrity Jessica Simpson caused a great deal of backlash from fans and critics. The media frequently skewered the couple, and the New York *Daily News* drew up this caricature of the two before the Cowboys were to play the New York Giants.

allowed to conduct 14 of them. The Associated Press reported on June 12, 2008, that Romo was working hard during OTAs. He told a reporter:

> You practice a lot of different shots in basketball—your fadeaway, your jumper. You practice a lot of different shots in golf. I find it funny most quarterbacks practice the same throwing motion. The reality in a game . . . your arm is going to be in different slots because you've got to throw around people.

Instead of trying to throw just as he had been trained to earlier, he was becoming more flexible. He wanted to practice more than the standard overhand throw that had been drilled into him when he came to the Cowboys.

The Cowboys won their first three games of the 2008 season. The wins included a dazzling offensive display by the Cowboys and the Eagles on September 15. Romo was 21 of 30 for 312 yards, but he had to bring the Cowboys from behind. They won 41-37.

On September 21, the Cowboys won their first game ever at famous Lambeau Field in Green Bay, Wisconsin. It was a kind of homecoming for Romo. The game was significant because the Packers double-covered Terrell Owens (put two defenders on him) and desperately rushed Romo throughout the game. So, Romo let his two running backs, Marion Barber and Felix Jones, do much of the offensive work, and his defense did the rest. The Cowboys won 27-16. Mark Maske wrote in the *Washington Post* that coach Wade Phillips told him, "Tony never ceases to amaze me. He has a will to play, and if things don't go his way early, he'll fight through it." Jerry Jones said that the Romo playing that night was not the same as the Romo who had played the previous season. He knew his limitations more. He let "his supporting cast step up and do it [win], and him to be a role player to some degree until his shots came."

The Cowboys lost a close game to the Redskins and won another close game against the Bengals. Their record was 4–1, and they had every expectation of going to the play-offs easily. Then disaster struck.

SEASON IN PAIN

The Arizona Cardinals changed their team personality in 2008 under second-year head coach Ken Whisenhunt. Their defense was now punishing, more physical than it had been. No one knew the team would end up in the Super Bowl later that season when the Cardinals played the Cowboys on October 12 at the University of Phoenix Stadium.

Romo was knocked down 19 times and was blindsided as well, but he brought the Cowboys back with 10 points in the last few minutes to tie the game. On the first play in overtime, Romo was hit, fumbled, and recovered his fumble in a swarm of tacklers. But something was obviously wrong when he got up. He would later find out he had broken a finger on his throwing hand. He should have come out of the game but decided to play through the pain. His grit was admirable, but the results were not. His next two passes were nowhere near their targets. The Cardinals took advantage of a blocked punt and won, 30-24.

Doctors told Romo he would be out at least a month. He said he hadn't missed even a practice since high school and he wanted to play. He tried, but gripping the football was so difficult that backup quarterback Brad Johnson came in for the next three games. The Cowboys lost two of those, bringing their record to 5–4.

It was little consolation, but after the Arizona game, Romo had 14 career games with more than 300 yards passing. That broke the old Cowboys' record that Aikman had set years earlier. It took Aikman 165 starts to get to 13 games with 300 yards. It had taken Romo only 32 starts. Romo's 2008 passer rating was 103.5, one of the best in the NFL. It was no wonder that Cowboy Nation couldn't wait for Romo to get back.

When Romo returned on November 16 against the Redskins, his finger was still in a splint, his passes floated and fluttered, and most came up short. His hand took a beating every time the ball was snapped. He was intercepted twice inside the Redskin 30-yard line. In the fourth quarter, however, he made a crucial first down with a shovel pass on a scramble, then a crucial touchdown pass to tight end Martellus Bennett, giving the Cowboys a 14-10 victory. The quarterback jumped for joy as he left the field.

Romo told writer Judy Battista, "We had to have this one. . . . It was an important situation where we could prove to ourselves that we could be resilient." She wrote, "The waiting for Romo is over. He is back and he has brought the Cowboys with him."

The Cowboys won their next two games, including a 34-9 demolishing of the Seahawks on Thanksgiving Day, bringing their record to 8–4. Then their schedule turned to some of the strongest teams in the league.

2008 SEASON ENDS WITH A WHIMPER

The makers of the 2008 schedule had not been kind to the Cowboys. They faced four powerful teams to end the season, the first of which was the Pittsburgh Steelers, on December 8, 2008. The Cowboys led 13-3 with just over seven minutes to go in freezing weather at Heinz Field. The Steelers' defense took advantage of Cowboy receivers running the wrong routes and Romo's inability to grip the ball firmly in the cold. They intercepted Romo twice, the second leading to a game-winning touchdown return. These same Steelers would win the Super Bowl in a few weeks with the NFL's best defense.

Romo had connected with Terrell Owens for 33 touchdowns since 2006, the most of any quarterback-receiver combination in the league. But teams had been covering Owens closely, often with two defenders, and Romo had used many other receivers. The Associated Press reported on December 13 that Owens's frustration about being left out of the offense at times had spilled into the locker room. Owens may also have thought that Romo and Witten were making plays not included in the playbook and therefore excluding him. Owens wanted the ball, and he wasn't getting it enough. He was returning to the T.O. that fans in San Francisco and Philadelphia, but not Dallas, had seen.

The Giants then came into Texas Stadium and sacked Romo four times, once so violently that he had back spasms and could be seen wincing in pain at the end of the first quarter. For the first time in his career, Romo was getting injured badly enough to affect his performance. His offensive line was no longer able to protect him well. The Cowboys were still able to beat the Giants, 20-8, but they then lost to the Ravens and the Eagles. The Ravens' Ed Reed intercepted Romo twice, and the Eagles' offense destroyed the Cowboys' defense, 44-6.

The Eagles beat up Romo so badly that he collapsed in the shower after the game because of bruised ribs. Reporters were pushed out of the way in the chaos. A stretcher was brought in, but Romo was able to hobble to the training room.

The Cowboys ended with a 9–7 record that was not good enough to get them into the play-offs. The team was in turmoil. Something was going to have to change. But Romo had not had a bad season—he had a 114.7 rating in the fourth quarter of 2008 games, among the best in the league. But his passer rating had dipped in the month of December to 67.9. That needed to change for him to be considered an elite quarterback.

JOINING FOOTBALL'S ELITE

On March 5, 2009, owner Jerry Jones told the Associated Press that the Cowboys "will move on with a new team—a new attitude—and into a new stadium." Terrell Owens was released

The 2008 Cowboys season ended in pain for Romo, who had previously not suffered from many injuries. The game against the Philadelphia Eagles (*above*) was especially brutal, and Romo collapsed in the locker room afterwards from bruised ribs.

by the Cowboys and signed by the Buffalo Bills. Jones made a point of saying the team would be more "Romo-friendly." And Romo's attitude was even more serious about getting better. He told Jaime Aron from Associated Press Sports that he knew he had work to do, on conditioning, holding onto the ball, having good footwork before throwing a pass, and more.

In 2009, the work paid off. That season Romo became the first Cowboy quarterback to take every snap during the entire season. He smashed record after record: 550 passing attempts, 347 completions, 4,483 passing yards, and eight games with more than 300 yards passing all became new Cowboy milestones. He became the first Cowboy ever to throw more than 20 touchdowns while throwing fewer than 10 interceptions. He was brilliant.

At 11–5, the 2009 Cowboys won the NFC East, and on January 9, 2010, they won their first play-off game since 1996. That day against the Eagles, Romo led his team to score after score, including 27 points in a single quarter. The Cowboys won, 34-14. He had never been better.

Just as his career had earlier seen a meteoric rise and then a terrible fall, the 2009 season ended with a thud. On January 17, 2010, Romo and his team went to Minneapolis to face one of his boyhood idols, Brett Favre, and the Vikings. Everything that went right the previous week went wrong that day. Romo's pass protection broke down again and again—he was sacked six times, fumbling three times. The Vikings raided the pocket and didn't let Romo escape. The Cowboys lost, 34-3, and their season was over. Romo was devastated but vowed that he and the team would learn and get better.

Romo had become a better and more mature team leader in 2009. When he went to his third Pro Bowl in late January 2010, he was considered by many to finally be an elite quarterback. He had passed for more than 300 yards in 24 games (the great Troy Aikman, by comparison, had 13 games over 300 yards) and had thrown for more than 4,000 yards in two seasons (2007 and 2009). Those are the numbers of a top-notch professional quarterback.

THE SNAKEBIT SEASON: 2010

Fans had great expectations for Romo and the Cowboys in 2010. But the dashed hopes at the end of the 2009 season continued into 2010. The Cowboys lost four of their first five games, each by a touchdown or less. Their defense was not as good as in 2009, but the offense attracted much of the blame. Romo had thrown only nine interceptions in all of 2009, but he had seven interceptions through the first six games of 2010. Many were passes tipped into the air by receivers and defenders and not simply his mistakes. And Romo actually had a career-best pass completion percentage (almost 70 percent) for the first six games. The Cowboys offense, though, stalled

THE GREATEST NFL QUARTERBACK OF ALL TIME

People love to rank other people. Perhaps that comes from our earliest ancestors, who needed to know who was best at hunting or fighting or finding food to keep the tribe alive. For whatever reason, sports rankings are endless.

One of the most popular is arguing over who is the best NFL quarterback of all time. Is winning a Super Bowl the most important thing? The first quarterback to win four Super Bowls was Terry Bradshaw, in a period from 1975 to 1980. Joe Montana won four in the 1980s. But if Super Bowl wins are the measure, Trent Dilfer, who won one Super Bowl in 2000 with the Baltimore Ravens, is a greater quarterback than Dan Marino, who didn't win any. Clearly, more than winning Super Bowls is involved in ranking.

How about just using the passer rating system and giving the crown to Steve Young with his career rating of 96.8? But those ratings partly depend on the type of offense the quarterback is in. John Elway is rated lower than many quarterbacks today, and no one leaves Elway out of the top 10.

How about most passes completed? Brett Favre leads at 5,377 (and counting), with Marino second at 4,967 and Elway third at 4,123. But that doesn't take into account winning and leadership. For just winning, Montana won 71 percent of his starts. Elway won 64 percent of his starts and Marino 60 percent.

too many times with turnovers and injuries. Romo told reporters that he felt "snakebit."

The biggest snake bite of all came against the Giants in Cowboys Stadium on October 25, 2010. Romo went back to pass early in the second quarter and threw a perfect strike to

ESPN.com asked seven NFL football experts with long experiences in coaching and evaluating quarterbacking talent to rank the best of all time. They took into account measurable aspects of passing: accuracy, velocity, and quick release. They also considered qualities harder to measure: toughness, football intelligence, leadership, and work ethic.

The results, posted January 28, 2008, by Mike Sando, had the following rankings:

1) John Unitas
2) Joe Montana
3) Tom Brady
4) Dan Marino
5) Peyton Manning
6) John Elway
7) Terry Bradshaw
8) Brett Favre
9) Otto Graham
10) Dan Fouts

But John Madden, whom many consider to be the most knowledgeable expert in professional football, says that Montana is the greatest without a doubt. Let the debate continue.

receiver Miles Austin. Giants linebacker Michael Boley, however, had a clear shot at Romo as he was releasing the ball—no one had seen Boley blitzing the quarterback. Boley slammed Romo to the turf, and Romo then lay motionless on his back and in obvious pain. He tried to catch his breath and even tried to get back in the game. But he was taken to the sidelines, and soon X-rays showed that he had broken his left collarbone (clavicle). Romo told reporters after the game, "I didn't know it was broken. I was kind of in shock." Soon he would be placed on the injured reserve list, and his 2010 season was over.

Then insult was added to injury. When Romo's replacement, Jon Kitna, showed a more vocal leadership style on the field, a war of words broke out among sports reporters about whether Romo was not only injury-prone but too laid back to be a great leader. ESPN's Tim MacMahon and Calvin Watkins, for example, debated online about whether Romo had a long or a short way to go to become a true team leader. But even MacMahon had to admit that "Romo has the most important attribute of a leader. He's a relentless worker, having never missed a voluntary weightlifting or teaching session during his NFL career." To his credit, Romo traveled with the team even while injured and took part in team meetings. But when Jerry Jones fired coach Wade Phillips on November 8, 2010, the losses to a snakebit season mounted.

THE QUEST CONTINUES

The trials of the 2010 season challenged Romo. But people are their best selves, their heroic selves, when they overcome challenges, set difficult goals, and try their hardest to achieve them. Romo has so far failed to achieve his most difficult goal of being in and winning a Super Bowl. Every NFL player wants the Ring, the trophy that makes all the effort and sacrifice worthwhile. Most players never win the Ring, but know that the quest for it is noble and worthwhile. They leave their blood and sweat (and tears) on the field pursuing not just

Since he joined the Cowboys, Tony Romo has grown into his role as quarterback and team leader. He continues to improve his game and, with his impressive statistics, will be remembered as one of the best quarterbacks in Cowboys history.

championships, but excellence itself. They sacrifice themselves (Romo has now had several major injuries) for a cause that grips both teams and fans.

And many NFL fans who will never root for a Super Bowl winner know that their team can still give them some of the happiest and most entertaining times of their lives. Romo's daring and creative play makes for pure entertainment and for magic moments that people can share for a day, a week, a season, and even a lifetime.

Romo now has an off-field partner to help in his quest for a championship and a more fulfilling life. He started to date KDAF-TV sports journalist Candice Crawford in 2009, and they became engaged on December 16, 2010. KDAF, a Dallas television station, broke the story the next day and showed a picture of the ring and the striking couple. They married on May 28, 2011, in Dallas in front of 600 guests, including Miles Austin and Troy Aikman.

Ramiro Romo told Todd Archer of the *Dallas Morning News* that he was proud that all of his children are "good people" with character, loyalty, and honor. Tony Romo has earned his father's respect and made his family proud. He has many different forms of love and affection surrounding and protecting him. He may or may not find himself with a Super Bowl ring, but he has already found what is most valuable.

TONY ROMO

POSITION: Quarterback

FULL NAME:
Antonio Ramiro Romo
BORN: April 21, 1980,
San Diego, California
HEIGHT: 6'2" (188 cm)
WEIGHT: 226 lbs.
(103 kg)

COLLEGE: Eastern
Illinois University
TEAM: Dallas Cowboys
(2003–present)

YEAR	TEAM	G	COMP	ATT	PCT	YD	Y/A	TD	INT
2003	Cowboys	0	—	—	—	—	—	—	—
2004	Cowboys	6	—	—	—	—	—	—	—
2005	Cowboys	16	—	—	—	—	—	—	—
2006	Cowboys	16	220	337	65.3	2,903	8.6	19	13
2007	Cowboys	16	335	520	64.4	4,211	8.1	36	19
2008	Cowboys	13	276	450	61.3	3,448	7.7	26	14
2009	Cowboys	16	347	550	63.1	4,483	8.2	26	9
2010	Cowboys	6	148	213	69.5	1,605	7.5	11	7
TOTALS:		89	1,326	2,070	64.1	16,650	8.0	118	62

(continues)

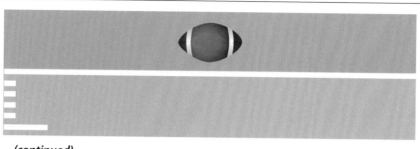

(continued)

RUSHING

YEAR	ATT	YD	Y/A	TD
2003	—	—	—	—
2004	—	—	—	—
2005	2	-2	-1.0	0
2006	34	102	3.0	0
2007	31	129	4.2	2
2008	28	41	1.5	0
2009	35	105	3.0	1
2010	6	38	6.3	0
TOTALS:	136	413	3.0	3

CHRONOLOGY

1980   April 21 Born Antonio Ramiro Romo in San Diego, California, at a naval base, to parents Joan and Ramiro Romo Jr.

1982   Romo family moves to Burlington, Wisconsin, where Tony grows up.

1996   Starts as quarterback for the Burlington High School Demons, named to the Wisconsin Football Coaches Association All-State team.

2000   Starts as quarterback for Eastern Illinois University and earns Ohio Valley Conference "Player of the Year" award.

2002   Named Ohio Valley Conference "Player of the Year" for the third straight year as quarterback for EIU.

   December Wins Walter Payton Award for best offensive player at a I-AA university.

2003   May 1 Signs $12,000 contract to play pro football with the Dallas Cowboys.

   August 9 First NFL action: preseason game against the Arizona Cardinals.

2004   August 21 Plays preseason game in Oakland, leading team to victory on last play.

2005   August Completes 23 of 37 passes in preseason for 237 yards.

   October 16 First official appearance in a regular season game other than holding for kicks, against Philadelphia Eagles.

2006   August 31 Gets $3.9 million contract extension and vote of confidence from Cowboys owner Jerry Jones.

   October 15 First regular season action other than holding for kicks or kneeling at end of plays, against

Houston Texans. First NFL regular season pass completion, to Sam Hurd for 33 yards.

October 29 First NFL start, against Carolina Panthers—Romo and Dallas win game.

2007 **January 6** First postseason action, loses game because of the Bobble.

February 10 Plays in his first Pro Bowl.

September 9 Beats New York Giants in first regular season game after the Bobble, 45-35.

October 30 Signs $67.5 million contract.

TIMELINE

1980
Born on April 21 in San Diego, California

2000
Starts as quarterback for Eastern Illinois University

1980

2002

1996
Named to the Wisconsin Football Coaches Association All-State team

2002
Wins Walter Payton Award for best offensive player at a I-AA university

2008   **January 13** Plays in first divisional championship game, loses to Giants 21-17.

February 10 Starts in Pro Bowl.

November 16 Returns from hand injury and leads team to victory over Washington Redskins, 14-10.

2009   First quarterback in Cowboy history to take every snap during the season. Sets team records for passing attempts, completions, passing yards, and number of games over 300 yards passing.

2010   **January 9** Leads Cowboys to first play-off victory since 1996, over Eagles, 34-14.

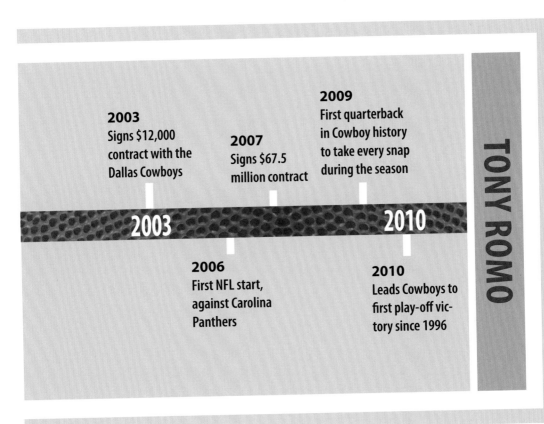

2003
Signs $12,000 contract with the Dallas Cowboys

2007
Signs $67.5 million contract

2009
First quarterback in Cowboy history to take every snap during the season

2003

2010

2006
First NFL start, against Carolina Panthers

2010
Leads Cowboys to first play-off victory since 1996

TONY ROMO

January 17 Sacked six times in loss to Vikings, 34-3.

October 25 His 2010 season ends when he breaks his left collarbone after being tackled by Giants linebacker Michael Boley.

2011   May 28 Marries Candice Crawford, a sports journalist for KDAF-TV in Dallas.

GLOSSARY

American Football Conference (AFC)   One of the two conferences in the National Football League, consisting of 16 teams.

balanced offense   When a team runs roughly half of the time and throws the other half, its offense is said to be balanced. A truly balanced offense means that the defense has no ability to accurately predict when an offense is going to run or pass.

blindsided   Hit from behind without warning.

blitz   A defensive play in which the linebackers or defensive backs give up their normal responsibilities to run into the offensive team's backfield to disrupt the called play.

carry   A run with the ball, also known as a rush or rushing attempt.

center   The offensive player who gets the ball to the quarterback, punter, or holder at the start of each play.

Combine   Professional teams invite roughly 300 of the best college players to an organized tryout camp, called the National Invitational Camp, or simply "the Combine."

completion   A pass caught by a receiver.

cornerback   A defender usually at the edges of the defensive secondary whose primary job is to prevent wide receivers from catching passes. Also called a "corner," this defender tries to stop runs to the outside and may blitz the quarterback as well.

defensive back   Any player in the defensive secondary, as opposed to the defensive line or a linebacker. The player's primary goal is to prevent receivers from catching passes.

down   One play. Each team has four downs to gain 10 yards.

draft   The selection of collegiate players by National Football League teams.

drive   A series of plays by the offensive team that begins when it gets the ball and ends when it scores or turns the ball over to the other team.

drop back   Movement backward by the quarterback after taking the snap to get ready to pass. Drop backs are usually one, three, or five steps.

end zone   The scoring area between the goal line and the end line, bounded by the sidelines.

field goal   A three-point score made when a player kicks the ball through the opposing team's goalposts.

first down   The first play of a series of four downs. The offense has four downs to gain 10 or more yards.

fourth down   The final play of a series of four downs, when the offense has to decide to try for a first down, attempt to score, or punt the ball to the opposing team.

free agent   A professional player not under contract.

fumble   A loss of control of the football by any player carrying it during a live play. Either team may recover a fumble, and the recovering team gains possession of the ball.

goal line   The line at the front of the end zone. A touchdown is scored when the football breaks the plane of the front of the opposing team's goal line between the two sidelines.

handoff   The action of a player giving the ball to a teammate, as opposed to throwing the ball.

holder   The player who receives the snap and places the ball upright on the ground for the kicker attempting a field goal or an extra point.

huddle   An on-field team meeting regarding the next play or plays. Usually the quarterback calls or relays the play in the offensive huddle, and the middle linebacker calls or relays the play in the defensive huddle.

incomplete pass   A forward pass that no receiver catches. Also called an incompletion.

interception   A pass that is caught by a defensive player.

kickoff   A kick that begins the game, the second half, the overtime period, and the series of downs after touchdowns and field goals.

line of scrimmage   A moving imaginary line that stretches across the width of the field to the sidelines and separates the two teams before the play begins.

linebacker   A defensive player usually lined up behind the defensive linemen and in front of the defensive secondary.

National Football Conference (NFC)   One of two conferences in the National Football League.

National Football League (NFL)   The largest professional American football league, currently consisting of 32 teams in two conferences, each with four divisions.

no-huddle offense   A tactic in which the offense quickly lines up without huddling before the next play.

offensive lineman   An offensive player lined up very near the line of scrimmage, usually a center, guard, or tackle; the player's job is to block for runners and passers.

off-season   The period between a team's final game and the beginning of preseason training camp.

onside kick   A short kickoff made by the kicking team with the intention of recovering the ball after it has traveled at least 10 yards.

overtime   An extra period added to a game when the score is tied at the end of regulation.

pass   A throw from one player to another. A forward pass goes down the field and a lateral pass (also just called a lateral) goes backward or parallel to the line of scrimmage.

pass interference   An illegal play by a defender trying to prevent a receiver from catching the ball, usually by hitting the receiver more than five yards from the line of scrimmage after the ball has been thrown but before it reaches the receiver.

pass route　　The pattern made by a receiver as he gets into position to catch a pass.

penalty　　A loss of yardage or downs or both by a team breaking the rules.

playbook　　The entire set of plays a team uses, traditionally in a notebook format.

play-offs　　Postseason games up to and including the Super Bowl. A team must either win its division or have one of the two next-best records in the conference to make the play-offs.

pocket　　The zone of protection for the quarterback behind the line of scrimmage that is formed by the offensive line and blockers when he drops back to pass.

practice team　　Also called the scout team, a group of eight players that each NFL team uses to practice with regular players during the week. The practice team cannot play in games.

preseason　　The period of time before the regular season during which teams train, evaluate players, and play exhibition games.

Pro Bowl　　The National Football League's all-star game.

punt　　A kick in which the ball is dropped and kicked after it leaves the kicker's hands. A punt usually occurs on fourth down and is designed to set the opposing team as far back as possible.

quarterback　　The player who directs the offense by calling or relaying the play and then receiving the snap and initiating a run or a throw.

quarterback keeper　　A designed play that calls for the quarterback to run rather than pass or handoff.

quarterback rating　　A number between 0 and 158.3 resulting from a calculation to determine a quarterback's passing effectiveness, taking into account completions, touchdown passes, interceptions, and other factors.

receiver   An offensive player who catches passes, usually either a wide receiver, tight end, or running back.

reception   A pass caught by a receiver.

redshirt   Term given to college athletes who delay game participation in their sport for roughly a year to extend their period of eligibility.

running back   An offensive player, also called a "back," whose main job is to run with the football and gain yards, block for other runners or the quarterback, or catch short passes. Halfbacks, fullbacks, and tailbacks are all backs with varying assignments, skills, and positions.

sack   A tackle of the quarterback by the defense behind the line of scrimmage.

safety   A defensive player who lines up in the secondary but often deeper than the cornerbacks. A safety is also a two-point score that occurs by tackling an opposing ball carrier in his own end zone.

scramble   A run by the quarterback out of the pocket to get away from tacklers while his receivers try to get open.

screen pass   A short pass to a receiver at or behind the line of scrimmage.

secondary   The defensive players who line up behind or outside of the linebackers. Also, the area of the field defended by these players.

shovel pass   A pass thrown with a backhanded or underhanded motion.

sidelines   The lines marking where the field of play ends and out of bounds begins. Also, the area just outside the playing field occupied by coaches, trainers, equipment managers, and players not in the game.

snap   The handoff or backward throw from the center that starts a play. The snap is usually to the quarterback, punter, or kick holder.

spike   Play during which a quarterback intentionally throws the ball to the ground immediately after getting the snap, to stop the clock.

starter   The player at a specific position who begins the game.

Super Bowl   The National Football League's championship game.

tackle   To bring to the ground a player who has the ball. Also, a position on both the offensive and defensive line.

tight end   An offensive player who lines up on the line of scrimmage next to the offensive tackle and is used as either a blocker or a receiver.

time-out   A break in action requested by either team or one of the officials.

touchdown   A six-point play in which any part of the ball crosses the plane of the opponent's goal line while in the possession of an inbounds player.

training camp   The multi-week period before the preseason, usually at a remote location, when players experience intensive physical and mental drills to prepare them for the exhibition games.

turnover   A change of ball possession because of a recovered fumble or interception.

two-point conversion   A two-point scoring play after a touchdown from the two-yard line during which a team successfully runs or passes the ball into the opponent's end zone.

wild card   A play-off team that does not win a division title but has one of the two next-best records in the conference.

yardage   Distance gained or lost from the line of scrimmage as a result of a play.

BIBLIOGRAPHY

Anderson, Dave. "Dallas Blossoming as Romo Absorbs Parcells's Wisdom." *The New York Times,* December 4, 2006.

Archer, Todd. "Dallas Cowboys' Romo Now Secure in the Pocket." *The Dallas Morning News,* October 31, 2007.

————. "Proud Family Present with Dallas Cowboys' Romo." *The Dallas Morning News,* October 30, 2007.

————. "Tony Romo. He's a Natural." *The Dallas Morning News,* November 25, 2006.

Aron, Jaime. "Romo's Aim: Better Shape, Smarter, More Leadership." *Associated Press,* June 17, 2009.

Associated Press. "Tony Romo Standing Taller in the Pocket." *The Sporting News,* June 12, 2008. Available online. URL: https://www.sportingnews.com/nfl/article/2008-06-12/tony-romo-standing-taller-pocket.

Battista, Judy. "Romo Comes Back, and So Do Cowboys." *The New York Times,* November 17, 2008.

————. "Romo Solves a Defensive Puzzle." *The New York Times,* November 12, 2007.

Bednar, Chuck. *Tony Romo.* Broomall, Pa.: Mason Crest Publishers, 2009.

Branch, John. "Now That Romo Has Rested, Critics Ask If He's Ready." *The New York Times,* January 10, 2008.

Cohen, Rich. "The Jessica Question." *Vanity Fair,* June 2009.

Crouse, Karen. "Given an Opportunity, Romo Has Breathed Life into the Cowboys." *The New York Times,* November 22, 2006.

Engel, Mac. *Tony Romo: America's Next Quarterback.* Chicago, Ill.: Triumph Books, 2007.

Fagan, Ryan. "Being Tony Romo." *The Sporting News,* August 7, 2007. Available online. URL: http://www.sportingnews.com/nfl/article/2007-08-07/being-tony-romo.

Flores, David. "Romo's Grandparents Revel in His First Game as Cowboys' Starting Quarterback." *San Antonio Express-News,* November 2, 2006.

Gardner, Howard. *Frames of Mind: The Theory of Multiple Intelligences.* New York: Basic Books, 1983.

Gay, Timothy. *The Physics of Football: Discover the Science of Bone-Crunching Hits, Soaring Field Goals, and Awe-Inspiring Passes.* New York: HarperCollins, 2005.

Lewis, Michael. *The Blind Side.* New York: W.W. Norton, 2006.

MacCambridge, Michael. *America's Game: The Epic Story of How Pro Football Captured a Nation.* New York: Random House, 2004.

MacMahon, Tim. "Tony Romo Has Room to Grow as Leader." ESPN.com, December 23, 2010.

Macur, Juliet. "Romo Shows Resiliency to Overcome Mistakes and Criticism." *The New York Times,* October 14, 2007.

Maske, Mark. "Romo Has Reason to Smile; Pressure Rises with QB's Stature, but All Is Well With 3–0 Cowboys." *The Washington Post,* September 23, 2008.

———. *War Without Death: A Year of Extreme Competition in Pro Football's NFC East.* New York: The Penguin Press, 2007.

Moe, Doug. "Simpson, Romo Find Fans in Wisconsin," Madison.com, June 30, 2008.

Nava, Carlos. "Cowboys' Romo Is Star in Their Sky." Cowboysplus.com, December 25, 2006.

Paolantonio, Sal. *How Football Explains America.* Chicago, Ill.: Triumph Books, 2008.

Rhoden, William. "Giants Could Give Romo an Early Return to the Beach." *The New York Times,* January 13, 2008.

Sando, Mike. "The Best Quarterbacks." ESPN.com, January 30, 2008.

Spousta, Tom. "After Soaring to the Top, Romo Tumbles Back to Earth." *The New York Times,* January 5, 2007.

Townsend, Brad. "Favorite Son: Hometown Cheers Romo's Rise." *The Dallas Morning News,* October 29, 2006.

———. "Tony Romo Learned the Price of Success." *The Dallas Morning News,* January 4, 2007.

Watkins, Calvin. "Tony Romo Has Improved as a Leader." ESPN.com, December 23, 2010.

Weir, Tom. "Romo Fever Burns Up Dallas as New QB Faces Lofty Expectations." *USA Today,* December 1, 2006.

FURTHER READING

Aron, Jaime. *Dallas Cowboys: The Complete Illustrated History.* Minneapolis, Minn.: MVP Books, 2010.

Freeman, Mike. *Bloody Sundays: Inside the Dazzling, Rough-and-Tumble World of the NFL.* New York: HarperCollins, 2003.

Garrison, Walt. *"Then Landry Said to Staubach . . .": The Best Dallas Cowboys Stories Ever Told.* Chicago, Ill.: Triumph Books, 2007.

Grabowski, John F. *Great Sports Teams: The Dallas Cowboys.* San Diego: Lucent Books, 2002.

Hawkes, Brian. *The History of the Dallas Cowboys.* Mankato, Minn.: Creative Education, 2004.

Housewright, Ed. *100 Things Cowboys Fans Should Know & Do Before They Die.* Chicago, Ill.: Triumph Books, 2008.

Luksa, Frank. *Cowboys Essential: Everything You Need to Know to Be a Real Fan!* Chicago, Ill.: Triumph Books, 2006.

Monk, Cody. *Legends of the Dallas Cowboys.* Champaign, Ill: Sports Publishing LLC, 2004.

NFL editors. *The Official NFL Record and Fact Book, 2009.* New York: Time Inc. Home Entertainment, 2009.

Stewart, Mark. *The Dallas Cowboys: A Team Spirit Book.* Chicago: Norwood House, 2007.

Taylor, Jean-Jacques. *Game of My Life: Memorable Stories from Cowboys Football.* Champaign, Ill: Sports Publishing LLC, 2006.

Towle, Michael. *Roger Staubach: Captain America.* Nashville, Tenn: Cumberland House, 2002.

WEB SITES

Official Web site of Dallas Cowboys
http://www.dallascowboys.com

Official Web site of the National Football League

http://www.nfl.com

Official Web site of Tony Romo

http://www.tonyromo9.com

Pro Football Reference: Tony Romo

http://www.pro-football-reference.com/players/RomoTo00.htm

INDEX

ABOUT THE AUTHOR

CLIFFORD W. MILLS is an adjunct faculty member at Columbia College in Jacksonville, Florida. An editor and writer who specializes in biographies of world leaders and sports figures, he is a lifelong football fan who roots for both the home team and the New England Patriots.